U.S. Debt

$800,000+ per Family? Trillions? Quadrillions?

Iris Marie Mack, PhD, EMBA

Jiayi Chen, MS

Junbo Zhu, MS

ISBN-10: 1973722216

ISBN-13: 978-1973722212

Disclaimer

Contents

Preface

Did you know that given the current financial standing of the biggest banks in the U.S., the country is quickly moving towards a possible financial Armageddon?

0.1 Assets and Derivatives Liabilities of Top Five U.S. Banks

As of December 2016, the top five U.S. banks were collectively exposed to approximately $200 trillion dollars worth of derivatives contracts. Table 0.1 shows the total assets and total derivatives liabilities of these top five banks. It's clear these banks have much more derivatives exposure on their financial statements relative to the amount of their assets. We will examine the data in Table 0.1 more closely in Chapter 6. (Hull, 2014), (Snyder, 2015), (Mack, 2016)

Table 0.1: Assets and Derivatives Liabilities of Top Five U.S. Banks

	Total Assets	Total Exposure to Derivatives
JP Morgan Chase	$2,490, 972	$46,992,293
Bank of America	$2,189,266	$33,132,582
Citibank	$1,792,077	$47,092,584
Goldman Sachs	$860,185	$41,227,878
Morgan Stanley	$814,949	$28,569,553

0.2 Derivatives and the 2008 Financial Crisis

For those of you who may not know what derivatives are, they are described as follows:

> *A **derivative** is a type of financial security whose price is dependent upon or derived from the value or return of one or more assets. The assets that provide the pricing base for a derivative are defined as the underlying assets of the derivative.* (Mack, 2014), (Mack, 2016)

In simple terms, a derivative is an economic tool that can be utilized to efficiently regulate – or in some cases, even manipulate – markets. However, since the value of a derivative depends on the value fluctuations of the underlying asset(s) and several other primary factors, the phenomenon takes the shape of a gamble where its efficacy and long-term impacts depend upon the likelihood of certain events occurring. (Folger, 2017), (Thomsett, 2013)

In the past, an immoderate use of derivatives has led to catastrophic economic collapse – who doesn't remember the 2008 financial crisis – the time when the global economy plunged straight into the pits of recessions? As discussed in Chapter 7, many experts blamed the derivatives exposure for the devastation that followed in the U.S. and around the globe. (Financial Crisis Inquiry Commission, 2011)

0.3 Impending Financial Crisis

Today, similar to the way things were back then, the U.S. economy is once again moving towards an impending financial crisis – at least the experts believe so – and they have good reason for it: The financial markets entered 2016 with the five largest banks in the country alone accounting for over $200 trillion worth of exposure to derivative contracts. The situation since then hasn't improved much. (Table 0.1)

To evaluate the current standing of banks in the country, we ranked the top 100 U.S. banks based on their total assets. This ranking unveiled a series of findings; including the facts that these banks are operating on incredibly high Price/Earnings (P/E) ratios, with a majority of them displaying an equally high Debt/Equity (D/E) ratio, coupled with low or, sometimes, even negative Earnings per Share (EPS). We will be taking a detailed look at the assets and liabilities of the top 100 U.S. banks in Chapter 6. (Piper, 2010)

Consequently, in Chapter 6 we also examine the Federal Reserve Bank's balance sheet. What one sees is as unsettling as the standing of commercial banks. Now, most of you may be aware of the fact that deposits essentially meet most of the criteria defined for debt. So, if we want to narrow down the definition of debt, we obviously have to consider closely the element of debt that ought to be included or excluded. (Griffin, 2010)

Ask an average American how much debt the U.S has accumulated over the years; they'll probably answer $20 trillion. After all, that's what they've been told, or have seen in the *U. S. Debt Clock*. In actuality, this amount may be significantly higher than what it is oft times stated to be. (U.S. Debt Clock, 2017)

Calculating the total U.S. debt is not that simple. There is a lot more that goes into it apart from the obvious economic indicators. The *U.S Debt Clock* may be able to provide us with a ballpark "figure" for the amount of debt the U.S. is currently under, but the extent of its accuracy is debatable.

To find out what construes as the U.S. debt, how it accumulated, who has to repay it, what is the total debt standing of the U.S., how it impacts the Federal Reserve and commercial banks, and what role derivatives play in its calculation – we will be exploring each of these elements one by one in this book.

For that matter, one must understand the workings of the *U.S Debt Clock*, and this is where we begin in Chapter 1.

0.4 Overview of the Book

Some of the key features of this book are the numerous references for further study, examples, illustrations and graphics. The structure of the chapters in this book is as follows:

Chapter 1: U.S. Debt Clock - U.S. Debt Clock, U.S. National Debt, Department of Treasury, Debt Held by the Public, Intragovernmental Holdings, U.S. Total Debt

Chapter 2: How Did the U.S. Accumulate This Debt? – Deficits, Federal Budgets, U.S. National Debt, Which Presidents Raised the U.S. Debt the Most?, Social Security Trust Fund, Global Reserve Currency, Budget Deficits, Debt Ceiling Limit

Chapter 3: Whose Debt Is It - Really? The Taxpayers? The Bankers? - Federal Debt Held by the Public, Intragovernmental Holdings, Foreign Owners of U.S. National Debt

Chapter 4: Debt Ceiling - Debt Ceiling, Statutory Debt Limit, Federal Debt Limit, Second Liberty Bond Act of 1917, Bipartisan Budget Act of 2015

Chapter 5: Interest on National Debt Approaching ½ Trillion Dollars per Year! - Dow Jones Industrial Average, Quadrillion, Derivatives, Interest on Debt, DJIA

Chapter 6: Broken U.S. Banks: Assets vs. Liabilities – Banks, Banking System, Federal Reserve, Commercial Banks, Investment Banks, Price/Earnings (P/E) ratio, Debt/Equity (D/E) ratio, Earnings per Share (EPS), Notional Amounts of Derivative Contracts, Assets, Liabilities, Office of Comptroller of the Currency (OCC), Bank for International Settlements (BIS), Banks' Derivatives Exposure, Too Big To Fail

Chapter 7: Derivatives – Futures, Options, Swaps, Derivatives, Non-binding contracts, Leverage returns, Exchange-Traded Derivatives Markets, Over-The-Counter (OTC) Derivatives Markets, Subprime mortgage crises, TARP bailout, Exter Pyramid, $1,500 Trillion Dollar Derivatives Bubble

Chapter 8: Will the U.S. Ever Be Able to Pay All of Its Debt? - Debt-to-GDP ratio, Medicare, U.S. Debt, National Debt

Acknowledgments

Dr. Iris Mack wishes to acknowledge the help of all the people involved in this book project.

- ❖ Co-Authors – Two of my former students and/or teaching assistants in my Energy Trading classes at the Tulane Freeman School of Business: Jiayi Chen, M.S. and Junbo Zhu, M.S.
- ❖ Professional Editor – Wayne H. Purdin
- ❖ Graphics Artist – Mohammad Asif of *JaZaa Financial Advisory*
- ❖ Professional Indexer – Jessica McCurdy Crooks of *Next Index Services, LLC.*

Without the hard work, patience, support, and dedication of these individuals, this book project would not have become a reality.

Chapter 1. U.S. Debt Clock

1.1 Overview of the U.S. Debt Clock

Log on to www.USDebtClock.org and you'll notice a "clock" that keeps ticking in an attempt to constantly update and track the national debt that according to the clock, currently stands near $20 trillion – something we previously discussed in the Preface. The same amount is updated daily on the Treasury Direct website of U.S. Department of Treasury, Bureau of the Public Debt - in the Debt to the Penny section. (U.S. Debt Clock, 2017), (Treasury Direct, 2017a), (Bureau of Public Debt, 2017), (DebttothePenny, 2017), (Watson, 1989)

Figure 1.1: Screen Shot of U.S. Debt Clock on June 13, 2017 (U.S. Debt Clock, 2017)

The *U.S. Debt Clock* is an independent entity that painstakingly provides U.S. taxpayers with relevant data pertaining to the *U.S. National Debt*.

The clock uses algorithms that calculate the approximate rate of change in the amount of outstanding debt between the daily updates posted by the U.S. Department of Treasury. (Amadeo, 2016), (U.S. Debt Clock, 2017)

1.2 Categories of U.S. National Debt

The *Bureau of Public Debt* calculates the *U. S. National Debt* figures after taking into account daily reports from all the major reporting entities, including the Federal Reserve Bank. This debt, the Federal Reserve Bank calculates, is the debt owed by the Federal Government. Essentially, this debt is divided into two broad categories: *Debt Held by the Public* and the *Intragovernmental Holdings.* (Federal Reserve, 2017)

Before we go any further, it is important to define what each of these terms mean.

National Debt

> The **national debt** *is the total outstanding borrowings of a central government comprising internal (owing to national creditors) and external (owing to foreign creditors) debt incurred in financing its expenditure.* (Business Dictionary, 2017)

Debt Held by the Public

> The **Debt Held by the Public** *is all federal debt held by individuals, corporations, state or local governments, Federal Reserve Banks, foreign governments, and other entities outside the United States Government less Federal Financing Bank securities.* (Treasury Direct, 2017b)

Intragovernmental Holdings

> **Intragovernmental Holdings** *are Federal Financing Bank securities and Government Account Series securities held by Government trust funds, revolving funds, and special funds. A small amount of marketable securities is held by government accounts.* (Treasury Direct, 2017b)

We will discuss the *Debt Held by the Public and the Intragovernmental Holdings* in further details in Chapter 3. In the meantime, now that we have the necessary definitions and an understanding of National Debt and its components, it's time to move on to the more important aspects of the subject. (Bureau of Public Debt, 2017)

1.3 Every U.S. Taxpayer Is Liable for $165,896 in U.S. National Debt

The questions that now arise are:
1. Whether it's $20 trillion or more, where did the *U.S. National Debt* come from?
2. How much are U.S. taxpayers on the hook for these trillions of dollars in debt?
While the first question makes an ideal subject to be covered in separate chapters (and we will be doing so in subsequent chapters) here's a hint for the average American: Do the terms *Federal Reserve*, *bank debt*, and *derivatives* ring a bell?

Now, let's take a look at the second question. According to the *U.S. Debt Clock*, every taxpayer of the U.S. is liable for $165,896 each in U.S. National Debt! *It's not us, it's the counters on the U.S. Debt Clock that says this.* (U.S. Debt Clock, 2017), (Figure 1.1)

1.4 Chapter Wrap-Up

In this chapter, we gave readers an introduction to the *U.S. National Debt* and some of the issues we wish to tackle in this book. To accomplish these tasks, we discussed:

- ❖ U.S. Debt Clock
- ❖ U.S. National Debt
- ❖ Debt Held by the Public
- ❖ Intragovernmental Holdings

If you look closely at the *U.S. Debt Clock* counters, you can see two different debt counts:

- ❖ *U.S. National Debt*
- ❖ *U.S. Total Debt*

You are already familiar with the concept of *U.S. National Debt*. In Chapter 2 we will be telling you more about the *U.S. Total Debt* and the difference between the two.

Chapter 2. How Did the U.S. Accumulate This Debt?

2.1 U. S. Total Debt

By the end of Chapter 1, we are all aware of the fact that when it comes to measuring consolidated debt for the U.S., we basically have two different measures. One of them is the *U.S. National Debt*, which is an accumulation of the *Debt Held by the Public* and the *Intragovernmental Holdings* attributed to the U.S. government.

The second measure is the *U.S. Total Debt*. Now if you take a look at the *U.S. Debt Clock*, you'd find that the *U.S. Total Debt* is considerably higher than the *U.S. National Debt*. The *U.S. Total Debt* is currently $67+ trillion dollars! This is because the amount of *U.S. Total Debt* includes *U.S. National Debt* with the addition of the amounts owed by everyone in the U.S. including the Federal, state, and local governments, households, financial institutions (mainly banks) and businesses in the U.S. (U.S. Debt Clock, 2017), (Figure 1.1)

2.2 The U.S. Total Debt per Family Is $812,932

According to the *U.S. Debt Clock*, the *U. S. Total Debt per Citizen* as of June 13, 2017 is $207,514. In addition, the *U. S. Total Debt per Family* as of June 13, 2017 is $812,932. At this rate, we will soon be crossing over the $1 million dollar mark for the *U. S. Total Debt per Family*. (U.S. Debt Clock, 2017), (Figure 1.1)

2.3 Relationship Between Budget Deficits and the National Debt

To be able to grasp the concept of debt accumulation or where it comes from, it is important to first understand how the federal government works. Like companies, governments too, adhere to annual budgets where they plan their expected expenditure and forecast the speculated income. Then reality strikes and things don't usually go according to the planned monetary policy. Every time the federal government ends up spending more money than it earns (through various income-generating activities), there is a *budget deficit*. (Bittle, 2011)

To highlight the relationship between *budget deficit* and national debt, we include the formal definition of *budget deficit* from Investopedia:

> *A **budget deficit** is an indicator of financial health in which expenditures exceed revenue. The term budget deficit is most commonly used to refer to government spending rather than business or individual spending, but can be applied to all of these entities. When referring to accrued federal government deficits, the deficits are referred to as the national debt. (Investopedia, 2017a)*

Now, to finance this shortage of funds the *Treasury Department* steps in and issues treasury notes, bonds, and bills to borrow the amount that would compensate for the deficit at hand. These financial instruments can be issued to everyone, including domestic and foreign investors (both individuals and corporations) as well as the governments of other countries. (Thau, 2010)

To sum it all up, when we refer to the *U.S. National Debt*, it is an accumulation of the annual budget deficits faced by the Federal Government. The same, when extended to and combined with borrowings from international-level organizations such as the World Bank or any other international private financial institution, is termed the *U. S. Total Debt*.

Since the beginning of the U.S.'s operations, debt has been a key aspect of ensuring that the Federal Government does not fail to meet its obligations to the U.S. Taxpayers. The year 1790 was the first time ever that the U.S. Government incurred debt on a National level after the Revolutionary War. (Investopedia, 2016)

Over the course of centuries following that, the U.S. debt has grown exponentially due to inflation, economic recessions, high unemployment, outsourcing, and wars. Today, as the debt stands, the U.S. Federal Government has been unable to limit its spending within the constraints of the national budget, which has ultimately led the debt amount to soar beyond control.

2.4 Which U.S. Presidents Raised the National Debt the Most?

So when we look at the *U.S. National Debt* that stands at almost $20 trillion, the first question that arises is: *How did it get so large?* There are several factors that contributed to this amount:
One key factor – as previously mentioned – is the accumulated deficits of the Federal Budgets. Presidents over the years have introduced various tax cuts and programs for public benefit that have only added to the previously progressing amount of debt the U.S. has.

To date, the biggest budget deficit is attributed to President Obama, with President Bush following close behind. In Table 2.1 and Figure 2.1 we provide some data for the national debt accumulated under the five U.S. presidents before President Trump entered office. Please note that we only present data for the amount of debt accumulated under these presidents – omitting the amount of debt accumulated during their first year in office. The reason for doing this is because presidents have very little control over the amount of debt accumulated during their first year in office. The budget for their first fiscal year is determined by their predecessor. (Amadeo, 2017e), (Clark, 2017)

Table 2.1 Amount the Debt Increased Under Five U.S. Presidents

President	Amount accumulated in 7 years
Ronald Reagan	$1.860 Trillion
George H. W. Bush	$1.554 Trillion
Bill Clinton	$1.396 Trillion
George W. Bush	$5.849 Trillion
Barack Obama	$7.917 Trillion

Figure 2.1 Percentage the Debt Increased Under Five U.S. Presidents

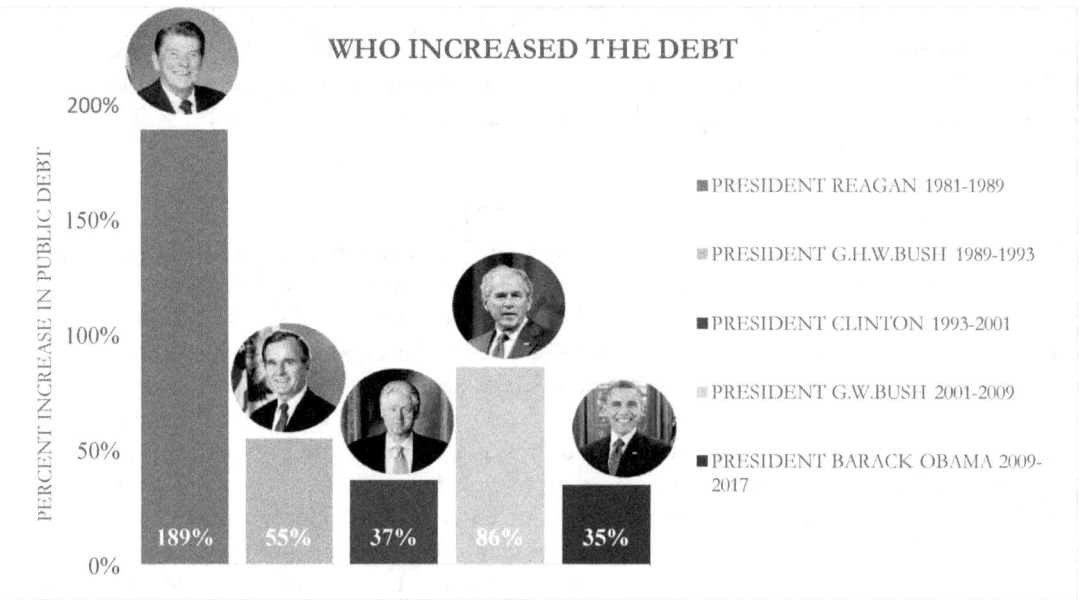

Source: U.S Department of the Treasury

Can President Donald Trump "make a deal" on America's debt? With President Trump in the White House, just how the U.S. attempts to get out of this debt mess would be the question. President Trump views himself as "the king of debt." Throughout his career, he has shown a penchant for utilizing the legal, banking, and corporate systems to his advantage to reduce his debt. Hence, it would be interesting to see how his plan for dealing with the U.S. debt unfolds. Will his plan be realistic? (CNNMoney, 2016), (Trump, 2015)

2.5 Borrowings from the Social Security Trust Fund

Another thing quite common among all previous presidents is the borrowings from the *Social Security Trust Fund*. The money in this trust fund was sourced from payroll taxes paid by hard-working Americans. This money belongs to teachers, nurses, bus drivers, retirees, veterans…. You get the picture. In an ideal situation, this amount should have been invested somewhere to be paid out to the people of America when they retire. Instead, it is loaned out interest-free to fuel government spending in Washington, D.C. When the U.S. Federal Government borrows money from the *Social Security Trust Fund,* it is not borrowing money from itself. It is, instead, borrowing money from you and me – people who entrusted the government with our money! (Davis, 2016), (Smith, 2015)

Since we're already at it, it's important to highlight the fact that lower interest rates on the securities issued by the Treasury Department, are actually in favor of the Federal Government. These lower interest rates allow the U.S. government to continue operating on budget deficits. If you're wondering why people still invest in these securities for lower returns, the answer is the perceived economic power of the U.S., which makes them believe the U.S. government has the ability to pay them back. So whether we like it or not, without too much fear of consequences, people and even foreign countries acquire these financial instruments, even in times of economic recession. (Amadeo, 2017a)

2.6 U.S. National Debt Owned by Foreign Countries

Coming to the international aspect of the whole scenario, another factor that impacts the amount of *U.S. National Debt* is countries such as Japan and China buy the U.S. securities issued by the U.S. Treasury Department to ensure the value of their currencies remain stable in comparison with the U.S. dollar. For example, the U.S. dollar is a significant foreign currency reserve to China. It keeps the Chinese RMB in a stable and containable fashion. More on the *U.S. National Debt* owned by China and Japan will be discussed in Chapter 3.

Despite the increasing amount of *U. S. National Debt,* these foreign countries don't mind lending to the U.S. because this ensures that we keep purchasing their products and services for years to come. However, over the course of the last two years, there has been a decline in debt holdings these foreign countries have held when it comes to the U.S.

In addition to all of this, the U.S. Congress decided to raise the *debt-ceiling limit* for the country, welcoming additional debts piling up to the already substantial mound of *U. S. National Debt.* What exactly is the debt-ceiling limit and how it affects the amount of National Debt and the consequent workings of the financial sector in the U.S. is something we will be discussing in detail in Chapter 4. (Amadeo, 2017a), (Hall, 2015)

2.7 Chapter Wrap-Up

In this chapter, we summed up how and why the *U.S. National Debt* keeps accumulating. To accomplish this task, we discussed the following:

- ❖ U.S. Total Debt
- ❖ Relationship between Budget Deficits and the National Debt
- ❖ Which U.S. Presidents Raised the National Debt the Most?
- ❖ Borrowings from the Social Security Trust Fund
- ❖ U.S. National Debt Owned by Foreign Countries

While we are already aware of what adds to the National Debt, a logical thought that might worry anyone privy to this information would be: *Who owes this amount? Whose debt is it?* If you've been thinking the same, it's about time you found that out in Chapter 3.

Chapter 3. Whose Debt Is It - Really? The Taxpayers? The Bankers?

When it comes to determining who owes the U.S. debt and who owns it, the situation is slightly more complicated than what one would expect it to be. Watch the American mainstream media news channels and they will tell you all about the amount the United States as a nation owes to Japan and China – $1.1 trillion and $1.06 trillion, respectively, as discussed in Section 3.3. However, these amounts alone are just parts of the greater $20 trillion debt we have been discussing thus far. (Amadeo, 2017c), (Mullen, 2016)

For the purpose of understanding who owes and owns the *U.S. National Debt*, we will be examining the following two basic categories of debt in sections 3.1 and 3.2, respectively: *Debt Held by the Public* and *Intragovernmental Holdings*.

3.1 The Debt Held by the Public

Recall that in Chapter 1, we defined the *Debt Held by the Public*. Let's take a closer look at this debt. According to the *Federal Reserve Bank of St. Louis*, the total amount of *Debt Held by the Public* is approximately $14.4 trillion. The *Debt Held by the Public* is expected to hit 77% of the U.S. gross domestic product by the end of this year - the highest level seen since shortly after the Second World War. In Figure 3.1, you can find a graph of the *Debt Held by the Public* from January 1, 1970 to January 1, 2017. (CBO, 2017), (FRED, 2017), (Meyer, 2017)

Figure 3.1: Federal Debt Held by the Public

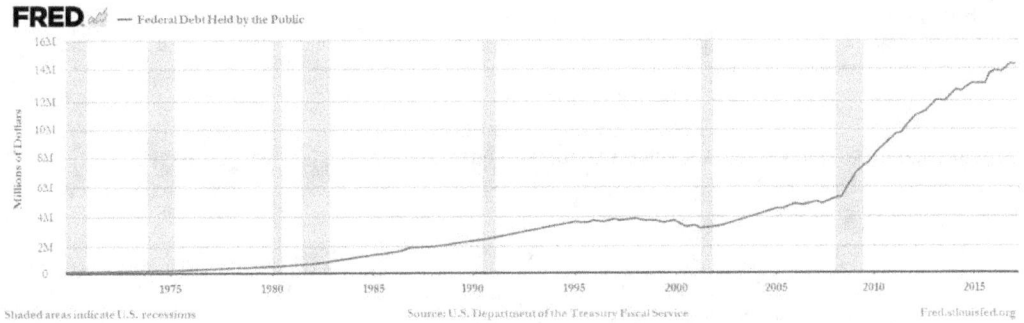

In Table 3.1 and Figure 3.2, we detail how the $14.4 trillion of *Debt Held by the Public* is broken down. We observe that nearly 45% of the total *Debt Held by the Public* is owned by foreign governments and investors – which we will discuss in greater detail in Section 3.3. (Amadeo, 2017c), (Factors Affecting Reserve Balances, 2017), (Treasury Bulletin, 2017)

Table 3.1: Breakdown of the *Debt Held by the Public*

Debt Holder	Amount of Debt
Banks	$570 Billion
Federal Reserve	$2.5 Trillion
Foreign (governments and investors)	$6.3 Trillion
Insurance Companies	$304 Billion
Mutual Funds	$1.4 Trillion
Private Pension Funds	$544 Billion
State and Local Governments (including their pension funds)	$874 Billion
U.S. Savings Bonds	$169 Billion
Others (e.g., entities such as individuals, government-sponsored enterprises, brokers/dealers, bank personal trusts and estates, corporate and non-corporate businesses, investors)	$1.4 Trillion

Figure 3.2: Breakdown of Debt Held by the Public

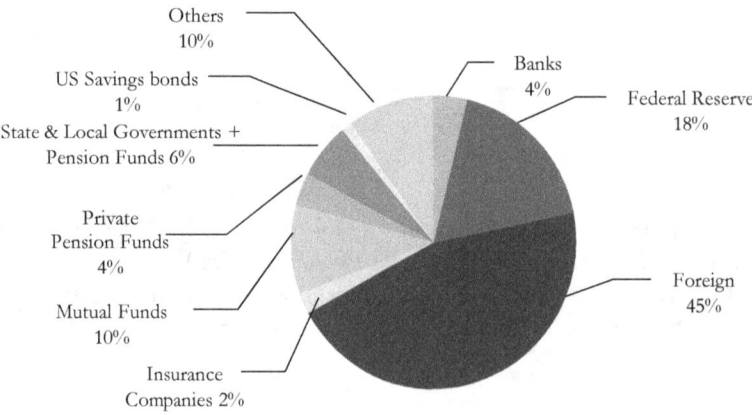

3.2 The Intragovernmental Holdings

Recall that in Chapter 1, we defined *Intragovernmental Holdings*. Now, let's take a closer look at this debt. *Intragovernmental Holdings* are also known as intragovernmental debt or intragovernmental obligations. Intragovernmental debt is incurred when the federal government borrows money from federal trust funds to help fund current government operations.

According to the Treasury Department, the *Intragovernmental Holdings* amounted to approximately $5.55 trillion as of May 2017. Essentially, this is money the federal government owes to 200+ federal agencies operating within the U.S. So, essentially, this is money the U.S. government owes to itself.

You are probably wondering how can the government end up owing money to itself? The answer to this is pretty straightforward. There are certain government agencies that end up generating tax revenue in excess of their current needs. Instead of holding onto the money, these agencies invest it in U.S. treasury notes.

Now, when the federal agencies purchase treasuries, the money spent on them accumulates in the general fund where it is utilized for government spending. However, holding treasury notes makes them eligible for redeeming the same for cash some day. When that day arrives, the federal government has to make payment to these agencies for which it will either end up issuing further debt or increasing the taxes.

In Table 3.2 and Figure 3.3, we detail how the $5.55 trillion of *Intragovernmental Holdings* is broken down. We observe that nearly 50% of the total *Intragovernmental Holdings* is owned by the *Social Security Trust Fund & Federal Disability Insurance Trust Fund*. (Amadeo, 2017c), (Clark, 2017), (Monthly Treasury Statement, 2017), (Treasury Direct, 2017c), (Treasury Direct, 2017d)

Table 3.2: Breakdown of *Intragovernmental Holdings*

Debt Holder	Amount of Debt
Cash on Hand for U.S. Government Spending	$580 Billion
Medicare	$294 Billion
Military Retirement Fund	$670 Billion
Office of Personnel Management Retirement	$888 Billion
Social Security Trust Fund & Federal Disability Insurance Trust Fund	$2.8 Trillion
Other Retirement Funds	$304 Billion

3.3: Breakdown of *Intragovernmental Holdings*

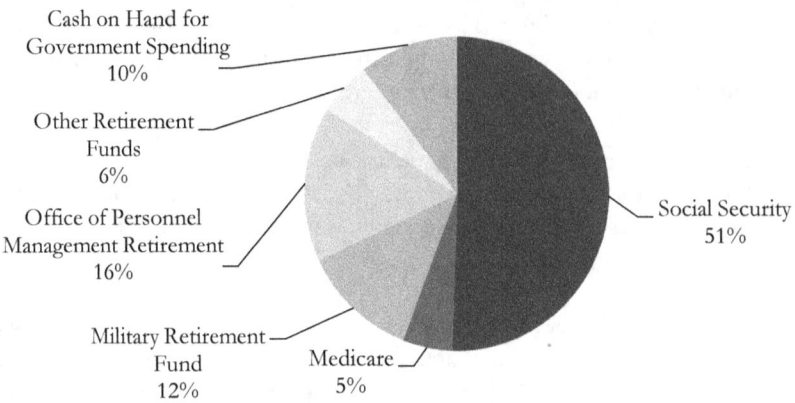

3.3 The Foreign Owners of U.S. National Debt

In case you're wondering about how much the U.S. owes to foreign governments, consider Table 3.3 and Figure 3.4. Here we present data for the biggest owners of the *U.S. National Debt* since February 2017. (Clark, 2017), (CNNMoney, 2016), (McCown, 2006), (TicData, 2017), (TreasuryDirect, 2017), (U.S. Debt Clock, 2017)

Table 3.3: Biggest Foreign Owners of the U.S. National Debt

Foreign Debt Holder	Amount of Debt
Belgium	$112 Billion
Brazil	$258 Billion
Cayman Islands	$258 Billion
China	$1.06 Trillion
Ireland	$308 Billion
Japan	$1.1 Trillion
Luxembourg	$217 Billion

Figure 3.4: Biggest Foreign Owners of the U.S. National Debt

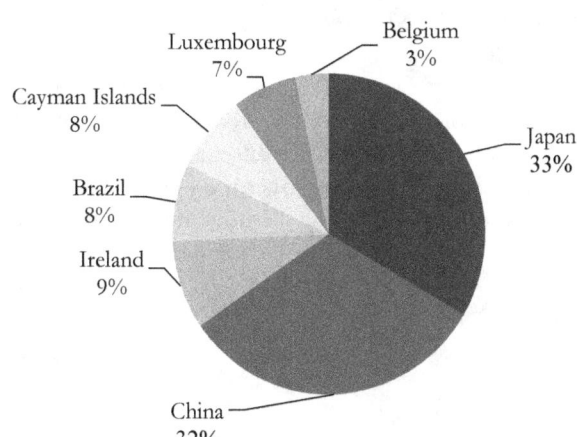

As indicated in Table 3.3 and Figure 3.4, Japan is the largest foreign holder of *U.S. National Debt* – closely followed by China. The United States collectively owes Japan and China approximately $2.16 trillion. These two countries have the obvious motive of maintaining the dollar value higher than their own currencies so that they can ensure the affordability of their exports into the U.S. market. It helps their economies grow. (Amadeo, 2017c), (Mullen, 2016), (TicData, 2017)

The next biggest foreign holders of the national debt of the U.S. are Ireland and Brazil who hold $308 billion and $258 billion respectively. Other foreign creditors of the United States include investors such as sovereign funds and corporations in the Cayman Islands ($258 billion).

Following Cayman Islands, other foreign creditors of the U.S. are Luxembourg ($217 billion), and Belgium ($112 billion). (Amadeo, 2017c), (Mullen, 2016), (TicData, 2017)

3.4 Chapter Wrap-Up
In this chapter, we discussed how the United States owes the most amount of money to its own people. To accomplish this task, we discussed and provided data for the following:

- ❖ Debt Held by the Public
- ❖ Intragovernmental Holdings
- ❖ Foreign Owners of U. S. National Debt

In the event of default, perhaps China, Japan and other foreign debt holders discussed in Section 3.3 won't be so happy with the U.S. However, it is the people living in the United States of America, who stand to lose the most.

Now that you are familiar with the facts and figures of who owns the debt that has been constantly growing bigger and bigger right in front of our eyes, many of you would question whether the system has enough checks and balances in place to limit the amount of debt the U.S. government has been issuing over the years. You remember we mentioned the *debt ceiling* earlier? It's time to revisit that topic now in Chapter 4.

Chapter 4. Debt Ceiling

4.1 Formal Definition of the Debt Ceiling

There's been a lot in the news lately about the *debt ceiling*. By the end of this chapter – and definitely by the end of the book – you should understand why. However, before we proceed to discuss the *debt ceiling,* let's first formally define it.

> *The* **debt ceiling** *is the maximum amount of money a country can borrow. It is also known as the statutory debt limit or the federal debt limit.* (Investopedia, 2017b)

For the United States, this debt limit was established by *the Second Liberty Bond Act* of 1917. The *debt ceiling* was initially conceived to actually make it easier for the U.S. government to borrow money. However, over the years, it has transformed into a political tool with potential to cause market volatility, defaults, and government shutdowns. (Dennis, 2017), (Kessler, 2013), (Firestone, 2014), (Sartre, 2017), (Sutch, 2017)

4.2 U.S. Debt Ceiling Data from 1990 to 2017

In Figure 4.1 we present *U.S. debt ceiling* data from President G.H.W. Bush's administration up to the beginning of President Trump's first year in office. (Dennis, 2017)

Figure 4.1: The Debt Ceiling (1990 – 2017)

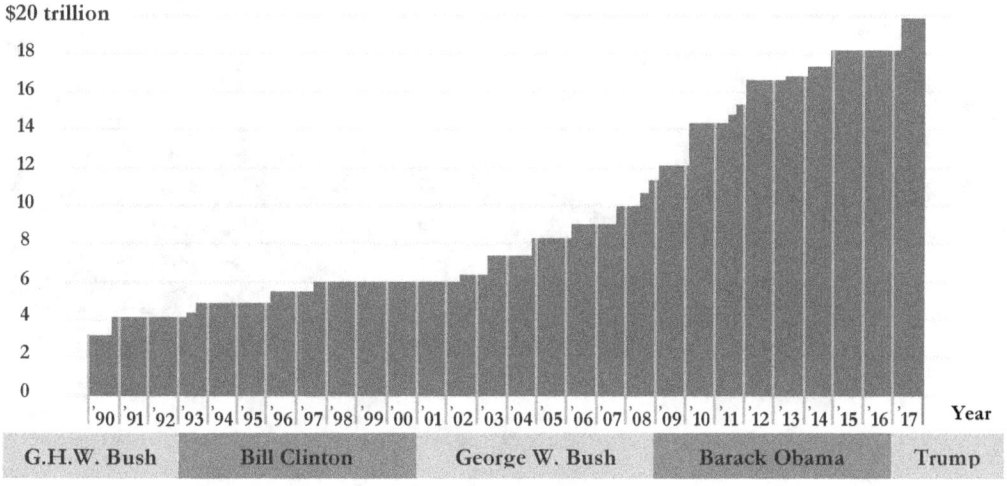

As denoted in Figure 4.2, a previous *debt ceiling* set by Congress was at $18.113 trillion. However, it was exhausted by the U.S. government on March 15, 2015. With more than a year to go until the election of President Trump, the Secretary of the U.S. Treasury under President Obama moved for the suspension of the debt ceiling on November 2, 2015 through the *Bipartisan Budget Act of 2015*. (Bipartisan Budget Act, 2015), (Smith, 2017)

The debt ceiling was intended to remain suspended until March 15, 2017. From March 16, 2017, the reinstated debt ceiling currently stands at $19.8 trillion. According to this debt limit, the *U.S. National Debt* should not go even a penny beyond this amount. In theory, the U.S. government is unable to go into more debt until the debt ceiling is increased. (ConcordCoalition, 2017), (Durden, 2017)

Figure 4.2: Debt Limit-Related Crises

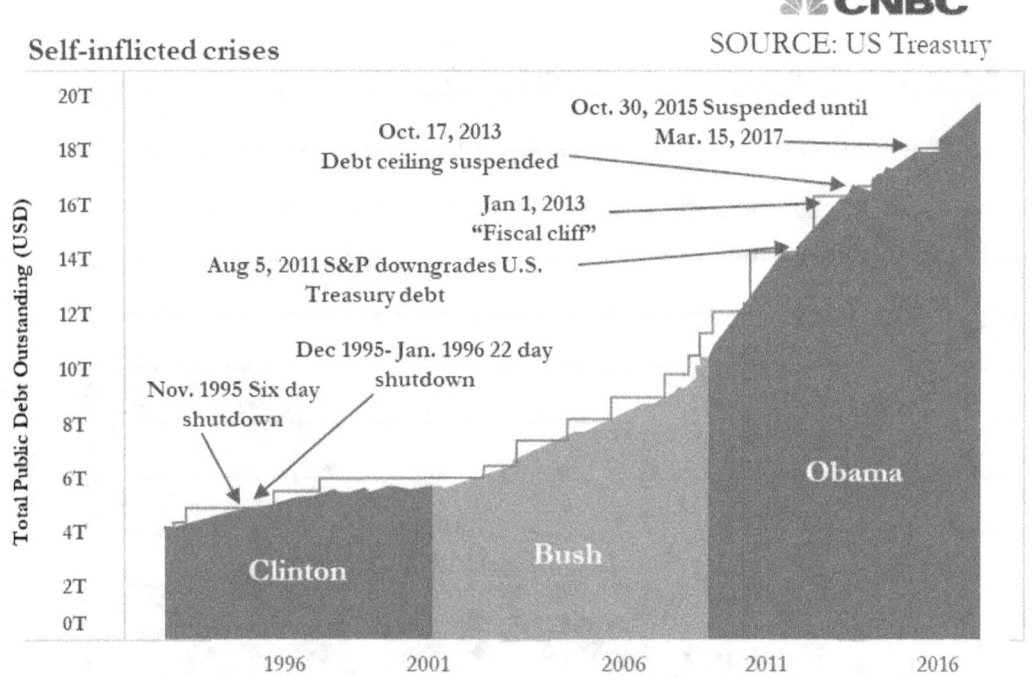

4.3 The U.S. Has Exceeded Its Current Debt Ceiling

According to the U.S. Debt Clock, the *U.S. National Debt* is $19.94+ trillion. (Figure 1.1) Hence, the U.S. has already exceeded its current *debt ceiling* of $19.8 trillion. Given the consistency with which the debt keeps increasing, it would be interesting to see how the Trump administration tackles the debt dilemma in the U.S. (Sartre, 2017), (U.S. Debt Clock, 2017)

Generally, the elected government officials are not in favor of decreasing government spending. As it is, this spending is used to finance programs that eventually benefit their donors and constituencies. Hence, in an attempt to stay in office and have a chance at possible re-election, a majority of elected government officials remain in favor of decreasing taxes and boosting government spending, which automatically leads to greater budget deficits and higher national debt.

President Trump however, has repeatedly discussed "draining the swamp" and decreasing government spending – something that has obviously attracted hostility towards him and his proposed policies. As of now, the U.S. Secretary of Treasury Steven Mnuchin has implemented "extraordinary measures" to pay off the public debt without borrowing any further amounts. (Savransky, 2017)

Given the current scenario, it doesn't seem likely that the U.S. Congress will vote on a higher *debt ceiling* without a major fight and Herculean efforts on behalf of the Trump administration. Hence, there are good chances that the debt ceiling process might just get delayed until the end of September 2017 to be conjugated with the annual budget. (Moore, 2017)

4.4 Chapter Wrap-Up

In this chapter, we discussed the U.S. *debt ceiling*. To accomplish this task, we discussed the following:

- ❖ The formal definition of *debt ceiling*
- ❖ *U. S. debt ceiling* data from 1990 to 2017
- ❖ The U. S. has exceeded its current *debt ceiling* limit

Chapter 5. Interest on National Debt Approaching ½ Trillion Dollars per Year!

5.1 Big "20" for DJIA and the National Debt

Earlier this year the Dow Jones Industrial Average closed above 20,000 for the first time. (Figure 5.1) As a result, Wall Street and the media were excited, and rightfully so – it definitely was something to be celebrated. However, when we look on the flip side, not much attention, let alone the same caliber of attention, is paid to the more important issues at hand – yes, we are talking about the *U.S. National Debt* of course. (Prestbo, 1999), (Crudele, 2017), (Imbert, 2017)

Figure 5.1 DJIA closed above 20,000 for first time on January 25, 2017 (Imbert, 2017)

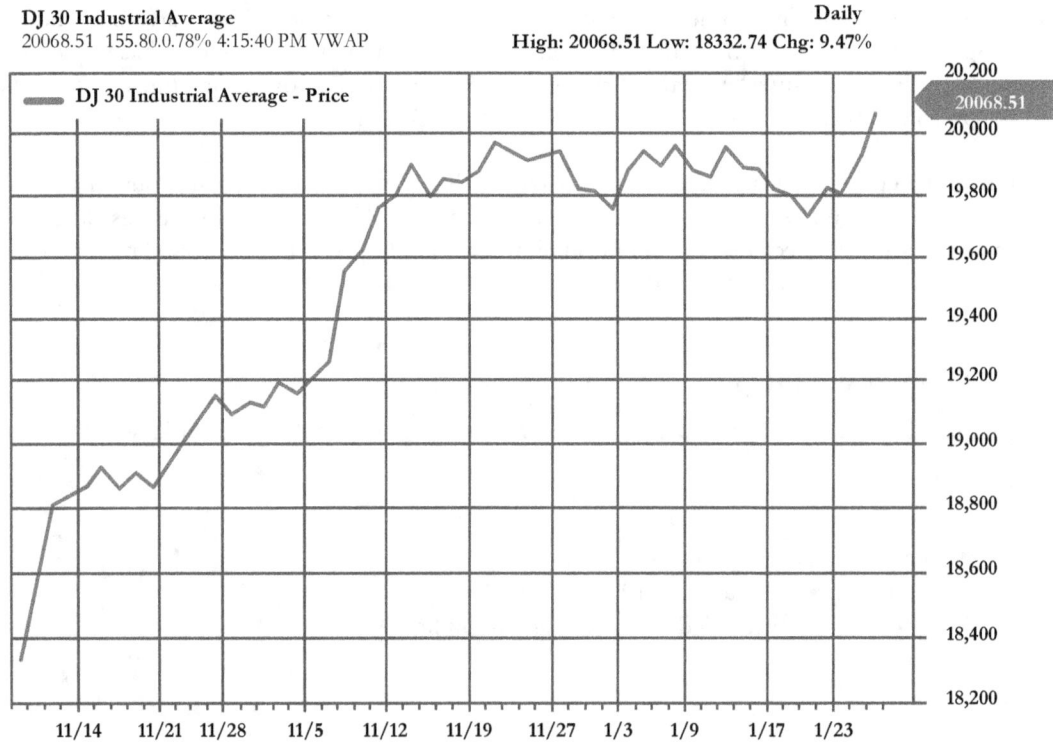

The coincidence is quite interesting: Dow Jones hit the 20,000 mark earlier this year and the national debt is set to cross a 20 of its own very soon. If nothing else, one thing is for sure, the U.S. is in a serious financial dilemma. Given the pace at which the *U.S. Debt Clock* is ticking right now, we might just hit $20 trillion by early July 2018. (U.S. Debt Clock, 2017)

However, if we look at it in realistic terms, there is still a lot of time to go before the dates on our calendars display JULY 2018; and in that time, there is a lot that can happen. While we spend time analyzing policies and debt figures, there may be people in the U.S. government thinking about the best possible strategies to efficiently cope with the debt dilemma as we know it – or maybe they aren't. One can never be completely sure.

When we say, "A lot can happen," we mean the pendulum can swing both ways. If the Treasury manages to bring in more revenue than it normally does, we may be able to slow down the debt clock. But if President Trump decides to proceed with his planned expenditures – such as launching his $1 trillion initiative to repair America's infrastructure and/or to build the Mexican border wall - we may be looking at an accelerated debt clock in the coming days. (Thomas, 2017)

One can even expect President Trump to continue his proactive approach at decreasing the *U.S. National Debt* the way he managed to do so in his first month in office, when the national debt amount fell by $12 billion. (Hoft, 2017)

5.2 Interest on the National Debt Is $442,565,594,766 per Year!

Unless otherwise controlled, the level of national debt is sure to increase higher than $20 trillion by the end of this year or early in 2018. As seen in Figure 1.1, on June 13, 2017 the *U.S. National Debt* as displayed by the *U.S. Debt Clock* was at $19.94+ trillion — rising continuously at an hourly rate of $13,404,542. That adds up to $321,709,008 million for ONE DAY! In addition, as denoted in Table 5.1, the interest per year on the national debt is approaching a half trillion dollars per year! (Crudele, 2017), (National Debt Clocks, 2017), (Patton, 2017), (U.S. Debt Clock, 2017)

Table 5.1 Approximation of the Interest on the U.S. National Debt

Time Frame	Interest per Time Frame
Interest per Second	$14,034
Interest per Minute	$842,040
Interest per Hour	$50,522,400
Interest per Day	$1,212,537,600
Interest per Year	$442,565,594,766

Obviously, things aren't as simple as displayed in Table 5.1. There's a lot that goes into the calculation and management of the national debt and interest. To make matters more complicated, the official debt statistics reported by the U.S. Treasury Department are not the same as those displayed on the U.S. Debt Clock.

Does that imply that one of these authorities is propagating the wrong figures? Probably yes!

And we think it's the U.S. banks that have a role to play in the slight discrepancy in amounts being circulated by these authorities. *You want to know how? Let's find that out in Chapter 6!*

5.3 Chapter Wrap-Up

In this chapter, we discussed how the interest on the *U.S. National Debt* is approaching a half trillion dollars per year. To accomplish this task, we discussed the following:

❖ The Big "20" for the DJIA and the U.S. National Debt
❖ The interest on the U.S. National Debt for various times frames

Chapter 6. Broken U.S. Banks: Assets vs. Liabilities

6.1 Economic Functions of Banks

For those of you who are familiar with the workings of the financial system in the economy, it wouldn't be difficult to connect the dots between the *U.S. National Debt* amount and the role banks have to play in it. For those of you who don't know why the financial system is an essential element in the workings of an economy, it is important to first understand the role of financial institutions in the U.S. (Rothbard, 2008)

In the simplest terms, banks provide a foundation for businesses and individuals in a country to deposit and/or invest their money. This money is then loaned out by the banks to the individuals and businesses that need it. The money banks lend out enables the public to make purchases – purchases that create the aggregate demand and supply that eventually drives the overall economy at various levels. (DR. ECON, 2001), (Fontinelle, 2017)

The structure of the U.S. banks is based on the Federal Reserve central banking system – as we will discuss in Section 6.2.

6.2 Federal Reserve

In the United States of America, the Federal Reserve plays the role of the economy's central bank. Established in 1913, the Federal Reserve overlooks the operations of 12 different regional Federal Reserve Banks that are located across the country in major cities. (Figure 6.1)

Figure 6.1: Twelve Regional Federal Reserve Banks (Federal Reserve, 2016)

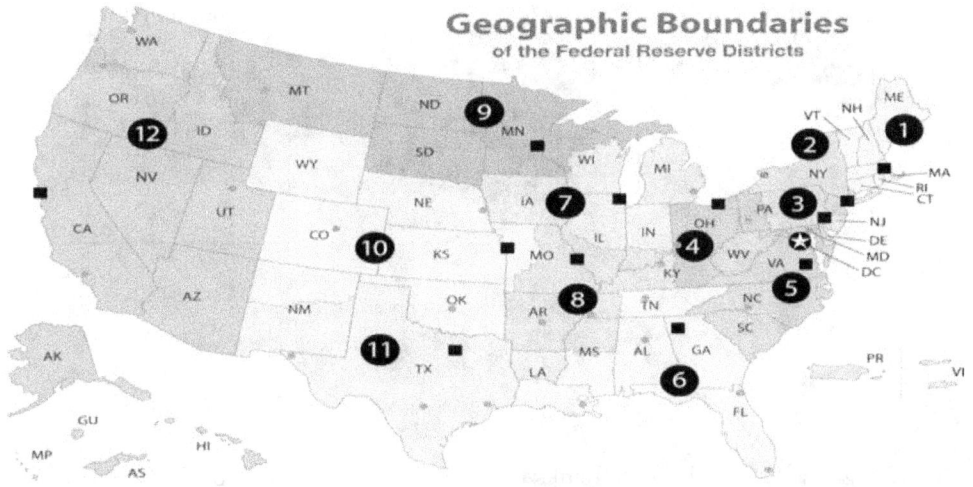

As discussed in (Mack, 2016), the Federal Reserve is an independent entity. The Federal Reserve even makes it very clear on its official website that it works as an **independent** entity, not controlled by either executive or legislative branches of the U.S. government. It also specifically states on its website, "It [Federal Reserve] is **NOT 'owned'** by anyone and is **NOT a private**, **profit-making** institution." ("Who owns the Federal Reserve?" *Board of Governors of the Federal Reserve System, 2013)*

The 12 regional Federal Reserve Banks operate more like private corporations with each having its own nine-member board of directors. Six of these directors are elected by the member banks of the respective Federal Reserve District and the other three directors are appointed by the Board of Governors. Most Federal Reserve Banks have at least one branch, and each branch has its own board of directors. Most of the directors on a branch board are appointed by the Federal Reserve Bank, and the remaining Branch directors are appointed by the Board of Governors. This Federal Reserve system structure is exactly the same as a private corporation. (Board of Governors of the Federal Reserve System, 2013), (Figure 6.2)

Figure 6.2: Federal Reserve Board of Director and Corporate Structure (Mack, 2016)

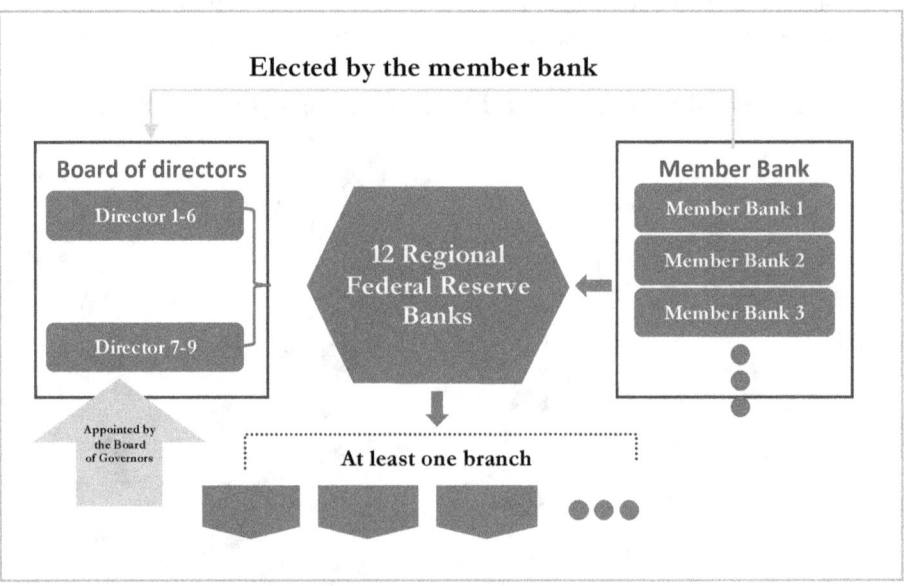

The 12 regional Federal Reserve Banks take care of a major chunk of the work for the Federal Reserve. These banks are responsible for generating their own incomes, which they do by providing the following sources:

➢ Interest received on government securities purchased for carrying out the work of the Federal Reserve.

➢ Interest earned from providing loans to other financial/depository institutions.

➢ Income generated from holding foreign currency.

The income earned through these sources is then invested to finance the everyday operations of these banks. These operations include gathering information and conducting economic research. The income in excess of what they require is then channeled back to the U.S. Treasury.

The *Federal Reserve Act* requires all nationally chartered banks to join the Federal Reserve system by purchasing the stocks of the Federal Reserve Bank for that district. But for the state-chartered banks, the Federal Reserve gives them the option to join the system, which means all the state-chartered banks can decide whether or not to become one of the "member banks" themselves. The amount of stocks that a member bank is required to purchase is proportional to the size of the bank. (Federal Reserve Act, 1913), (Mack, 2016)

We only introduce a few key points about the Federal Reserve Bank here. Please note that for a more detailed and in-depth discussion of the Federal Reserve please see (Booth, 2017) and (Mack, 2016).

6.3 Commercial and Investment Banks

Commercial banks and investment banks are two divisions of the global banking system. As you are probably aware, commercial and investment banks provide very different types of financial products and services. However, for sake of completion, we will include their definitions here.

A **commercial bank** is a financial institution that provides various financial services, such as accepting deposits and issuing loans. Commercial bank customers can take advantage of a range of investment products that commercial banks offer like savings accounts and certificates of deposit. The loans a commercial bank issues can vary from business loans and auto loans to mortgages. (Investopedia, 2017b)

An **investment bank** is a financial intermediary that performs a variety of services. Investment banks specialize in large and complex financial transactions such as underwriting, acting as an intermediary between a securities issuer and the investing public, facilitating mergers and other corporate reorganizations, and acting as a broker and/or financial adviser for institutional clients. (Investopedia, 2017c), (Krantz, 2014)

Because of the Great Depression, the *Glass-Steagall Act* was passed in 1933. This act authorized a complete and total separation of commercial and investment banking activities. However, the *Glass-Steagall Act* was repealed during the Clinton administration in the 1990s. Since then, banks have been allowed to engage in both commercial and investment banking activities under the same roof. (Benston, 1990), (Investopedia, 2015)

Commercial and investment banks operate on a microeconomic scale - focused on the market niches they serve. The Federal Reserve Banks, in contrast to them, operate on a macroeconomic level where they regulate the workings of all other banks.

6.4 Top 25 Banks in the U.S. Based on Total Assets

There is little left to the imagination when we talk about the *U.S. National Debt*, this book has been all about only that until now. Now obviously, the banks have a share in this national debt amount. In Table 6.1, we took the opportunity to rank the top 25 banks in the U.S., based on their total assets.

Table 6.1: Top 25 Banks in the U.S. Based on Total Assets

NOTIONAL AMOUNTS OF DERIVATIVE CONTRACTS (HOLDING COMPANIES)
TOP 25 HOLDING COMPANIES IN DERIVATIVES
DECEMBER 31, 2016, MILLIONS OF DOLLARS

RANK	HOLDING COMPANY	STATE	TOTAL ASSETS	TOTAL DERIVATIVES	FUTURES (EXCH TR)	OPTIONS (EXCH TR)	FORWARDS (OTC)	SWAPS (OTC)	OPTIONS (OTC)	CREDIT DERIVATIVES (OTC)	SPOT FX
1	CITIGROUP INC.	NY	$1,792,077	$47,092,584	$2,576,892	$4,200,083	$6,349,136	$25,140,908	$7,063,672	$1,761,893	$578,110
2	JPMORGAN CHASE & CO.	NY	2,490,972	46,992,293	1,725,732	1,612,075	8,601,365	25,670,787	7,353,940	2,028,394	497,996
3	GOLDMAN SACHS GROUP, INC., THE	NY	860,185	41,227,878	2,035,639	3,236,735	6,046,664	20,837,741	7,646,754	1,424,345	156,401
4	BANK OF AMERICA CORPORATION	NC	2,189,266	33,132,582	1,411,384	655,303	7,523,127	19,044,241	3,243,674	1,264,853	213,346
5	MORGAN STANLEY	NY	814,949	28,569,553	2,420,394	1,743,289	2,615,779	15,660,913	5,224,851	904,327	23,406
6	WELLS FARGO & COMPANY	CA	1,930,115	7,098,952	137,195	168,592	1,491,542	4,496,808	773,886	30,929	5,047
7	HSBC NORTH AMERICA HOLDINGS INC.	NY	277,783	6,342,537	803,267	479,694	620,478	4,012,446	301,625	125,028	34,562
8	MIZUHO AMERICAS LLC	NY	39,181	4,755,217	13,461	5,348	275,777	4,364,651	91,900	4,080	1,008
9	STATE STREET CORPORATION	MA	242,709	1,445,832	13,455	0	1,392,541	12,114	27,721	0	28,843
10	CREDIT SUISSE HOLDINGS (USA), INC.	NY	214,111	989,443	44,059	12,223	800,371	82,166	5,027	45,598	0
11	BANK OF NEW YORK MELLON CORPORATION, THE	NY	333,469	853,379	16,101	2,375	483,185	317,349	34,209	160	41,568
12	BARCLAYS US LLC	NY	204,485	724,366	28,154	230,193	293,321	18,130	40,920	113,648	0
13	RBC USA HOLDCO CORPORATION	NY	141,917	503,632	142,145	147,194	155,419	57,681	783	409	117
14	PNC FINANCIAL SERVICES GROUP, INC., THE	PA	366,872	409,473	40,317	30,545	30,462	278,642	22,782	6,725	1,380
15	SUNTRUST BANKS, INC.	GA	205,214	286,555	20,277	19,884	24,418	139,702	77,240	5,034	74
16	U.S. BANCORP	MN	445,964	280,377	7,417	0	50,814	181,360	35,715	5,071	1,913
17	NORTHERN TRUST CORPORATION	IL	123,927	279,007	0	0	263,845	14,056	1,106	0	11,677
18	TD GROUP US HOLDINGS LLC	DE	343,933	259,571	50,234	16,300	8,852	183,076	425	685	3
19	MUFG AMERICAS HOLDINGS CORPORATION	NY	148,144	176,966	6,396	0	93,439	68,922	8,198	10	462
20	DB USA CORPORATION	NY	186,603	175,290	4,633	105,147	44,544	12,381	5,323	3,262	0
21	BNP PARIBAS USA, INC.	NY	132,500	147,881	37	8,837	113,629	22,695	2,682	0	11
22	CAPITAL ONE FINANCIAL CORPORATION	VA	357,158	144,055	192	0	11,263	130,049	180	2,370	105
23	KEYCORP	OH	136,826	88,287	5,575	0	6,337	69,991	6,024	360	649
24	REGIONS FINANCIAL CORPORATION	AL	126,194	81,404	5,907	0	14,582	53,631	4,209	3,075	9
25	CITIZENS FINANCIAL GROUP, INC.	RI	150,023	80,398	0	0	9,473	61,096	6,916	2,913	58
	TOP 25 HOLDING COMPANIES WITH DERIVATIVES		$14,254,577	$222,137,511	$11,498,864	$12,673,816	$37,320,364	$120,931,534	$31,979,763	$7,733,170	$1,596,745

Note: Currently, the Y-9 report does not differentiate credit derivatives by contract type. Credit derivatives have been included in the sum of total derivatives.
Note: Before to the first quarter of 2005, total derivatives included spot FX. Beginning in that quarter, spot FX has been reported separately.
Note: Numbers may not total due to rounding.
Source: Consolidated Financial Statements for Bank Holding Companies, FR Y-9, Schedule HC-L

In Table 6.2, we present the P/E ratio, EPS, and D/E ratio for the 25 banks listed in Table 6.1. What we found most astonishing is that many of these banks had

- ❖ Price-Earnings (P/E) ratios that were high
- ❖ High Debt/Equity (D/E) ratios
- ❖ Low and sometimes even negative Earnings per Share (EPS)

Table 6.2: P/E Ratio, D/E Ratio and EPS for Top 25 Banks in the U.S. Based on Total Assets

Name	P/E	D/E	EPS (TTM)
CITIGROUP INC	12.86	229.27	$4.97
JPMORGAN CHASE & CO	13.28	244.63	$6.49
GOLDMAN SACH GROUP INC	11.78	461.38	$18.83
BANK OF AMERICA CORP	14.83	177.67	$1.58
MORGAN STANLEY	13.2	448.56	$3.37
WELLS FARGO & CO	13.47	175.49	$4.00
HSBC HOLDINGS PLC-SPONS ADR	114.67	213.33	$0.38
MIZUHO FINANCIAL GROUP-ADR	8.13	34.84	$0.44
STATE STREET CORP	16.53	82.07	$5.34
CREDIT SUISSE GROUP-SPON ADR	N/A	854.38	($0.84)
BANK OF NEW YORK MELLON CORP	15.35	144.16	$3.25
BARCLAYS PLC	22.26	283.02	$0.12
ROYAL BANK OF CANADA	9.66	228.41	$7.35
PNC FINANCIAL SERVICES GROUP	16.14	112.49	$7.59
SUNTRUST BANK INC	15.34	73.95	$3.66
US BANCORP	15.79	98.65	$3.31
NORTHERN TRUST CORP	21.64	91.02	$4.37
TD GROUP US HOLDINGS LLC	9.74	125.28	$5.07
MUFG AMERICAS HOLDINGS CORP	N/A	220.79	NA
DEUTSCHE BANK AG-REGISTERD	N/A	435.60	($0.85)
BNP PARIBAS	10.35	478.60	$6.72
CAPITAL ONE FINANCIAL CORP	12.36	127.25	$6.58
KEYCORP	21.56	96.42	$0.86
REGIONS FINANCIAL CORP	15.96	46.59	$0.90
CITIZENS FINANCIAL GROUP	16.68	86.84	$2.18

Note:
- **TTM denotes "Trailing Twelve Months"**
- **All data are from Bloomberg.com and WSJ.com**
- **Data extracted 6/16/2017 (end of trading day)**

MUFG integrated the U.S. operations of its subsidiary The Bank of Tokyo-Mitsubishi UFJ, Ltd. (BTMU) with those of San Francisco-based Union Bank, N.A.

TD Group US Holdings LLC operates as a subsidiary of The Toronto-Dominion Bank

Please note that for those of you who aren't familiar with the definitions of P/E ratios, D/E ratios and EPS, we include these definitions here for sake of completion. (Ittelson, 2009)

6.4.1 Price/Earnings (P/E) Ratio

> The **Price-Earnings (P/E) ratio** *is the ratio for valuing a company that measures its current share price relative to its per-share earnings.* (Investopedia, 2017d)

If we simplify it further, the P/E ratio basically highlights the amount an investor should invest in the company (in this case the commercial banks) to receive a dollar's worth of return from its revenue. Now, if we look at it from the investor's point of view, the P/E ratio shows the amount of money an investor is willing to pay for each dollar of the bank's earnings.

6.4.2 Earnings per Share (EPS)

> The **Earnings per share (EPS)** *is the portion of a company's profit allocated to each outstanding share of common stock. Earnings per share serves as an indicator of a company's profitability.* (Investopedia, 2017e)

The EPS is considered to be one of the most reliable indicators of a company's profitability. However, there is an important aspect of the determinant that is often overlooked by most: the amount of capital required in order to generate the net income (earnings) of the company.

You see, two different companies (banks in our case) can have the same EPS; the only difference is that one of them generates it with far less investment than the other. That company is, in this case, obviously more efficient in using its capital. Keeping all other things equal for both companies, the one with more efficient use of capital is definitely better than the other.

6.4.3 Debt/Equity (D/E) Ratio

Now you might be wondering how the above two measures relate to debt – the subject matter of this book. So let's first take a look at the D/E ratio:

> The **Debt/Equity (D/E) ratio** *measures a company's financial leverage, calculated by dividing a company's total liabilities by its stockholders' equity. The D/E ratio indicates how much debt a company is using to finance its assets relative to the amount of value represented in shareholders' equity.* (Investopedia, 2017f)

Considering that most of the banks in the U.S. show a high D/E ratio, the one thing that becomes evident is the fact that these banks have resorted to increased debt finance to fuel their aggressive growth. While the move may bring greater earnings than usual, it is still associated with higher levels of risks.

6.4.4. Analysis of the P/E Ratio, EPS and D/E Ratio for Top 25 Banks

Now if we look at the overall situation of our banks, their performance ratios provide contradictory information. Low or negative EPS shows that these banks are bad investments, but they have great price-earnings ratios that project further growth. To top it off, the debt/equity ratios are high. If there is anything that is certain, it's the fact that these banks aren't utilizing their debt finance efficiently.

Now there's a catch to that too. You see, the deposits we make in commercial banks check off most of the requirements of "debt" for the banks. However, at the same time, these deposits are used to generate further income for the banks and their clients (*could they be termed as assets in that case?*).

6.5 Analysis of the Federal Reserve's Balance Sheet

With the commercial banks not showing a bright prospect when it comes to their financial standings, the Federal Reserve Bank's balance sheet is no different. While analyzing these statements, we find the total liability is around 92% of its total assets. Treasury securities and swaps are about 58% of its total assets. Please refer to the extract in Figure 6.3.

Figure 6.3: Federal Reserve's Balance Sheet

		2016	2015
ASSETS			
Gold certificates		$ 11,037	$ 11,037
Special drawing rights certificates		5,200	5,200
Coin		1,873	1,890
Loans	Note 4	63	115
System Open Market Account	Note 5		
Treasury securities, net (of which $25,195 and $18,960 is lent as of December 31, 2016 and 2015, respectively)		2,567,422	2,580,676
Government-sponsored enterprise debt securities, net (of which $44 and $146 is lent as of December 31, 2016 and 2015, respectively)		16,648	33,748
Federal agency and government-sponsored enterprise mortgage-backed securities, net		1,795,003	1,800,449
Foreign currency denominated investments, net		19,442	19,567
Central bank liquidity swaps		5,563	997
Accrued interest receivable		25,598	25,418
Other assets		8	14
Investments held by consolidated variable interest entity (of which $1,742 and $1,778 is measured at fair value as of December 31, 2016 and 2015, respectively)	Note 6	1,742	1,778
Bank premises and equipment, net	Note 7	2,564	2,603
Items in process of collection		118	210
Other assets		1,056	1,063
Total assets		$ 4,453,337	$ 4,484,765

LIABILITIES AND CAPITAL

Federal Reserve notes outstanding, net			$ 1,462,939	$ 1,379,551
System Open Market Account:	Note 5			
Securities sold under agreements to repurchase			725,210	712,401
Other liabilities			1,012	508
Liabilities of consolidated variable interest entity (of which $32 and $21 is measured				
at fair value as of December 31, 2016 and 2015, respectively)	Note 6		33	57
Deposits:				
Depository institutions			1,759,675	1,977,166
Treasury, general account			399,190	333,447
Other deposits			58,413	36,532
Interest payable to depository institutions and others			403	252
Accrued benefit costs	Notes 9 and 10		3,118	2,892
Deferred credit items			922	246
Accrued remittances to the Treasury			1,725	1,953
Other liabilities			255	252
Total liabilities			4,412,895	4,445,257
Capital paid-in			30,442	29,508
Surplus (including accumulated other comprehensive loss of $3,985 and $3,802 at December 31,				
2016 and 2015, respectively)			10,000	10,000
Total capital			40,442	39,508
Total liabilities and capital			$ 4,453,337	$ 4,484,765

6.6 Derivatives: Cause of the Proliferation of Debt in the U.S. Banking System

So what explains this proliferation of debt in the U.S. banking institutions? According to the Office of Comptroller of the Currency (OCC, 2017), it's the outstanding derivatives contracts. As seen in Table 6.3 and discussed in the Preface, the top banks in the U.S. have sky-high amounts of outstanding derivatives contracts. These five banks collectively have derivatives contracts worth approximately $200 trillion dollars - almost 10 times as much as the total size of the *U.S National Debt!* (Snyder, 2015), (Mack, 2016), (LeBor, 2014), (BIS, 2017)

Table 6.3: Assets and Derivatives Liabilities of Top 5 U.S. Banks

	Total Assets	Total Exposure to Derivatives
JP Morgan Chase	$2,490, 972	$46,992,293
Bank of America	$2,189,266	$33,132,582
Citibank	$1,792,077	$47,092,584
Goldman Sachs	$860,185	$41,227,878
Morgan Stanley	$814,949	$28,569,553

Now, considering the fact that derivatives played a pivotal role in the global financial crisis that hit the world back in 2008, the situation today is quite similar – or perhaps far more lethal. The top four U.S. banks today are nearly 40% larger than they were back in 2008 – but that's only the beginning.

The point of concern is that as these banks grow in size, so does their debt and the economy's dependability on them. At this point, 42% of all the loans in the country are held by the five largest U.S. banks; and, to make matters worse, the top six hold almost 67% of the total assets in the country's financial system. (Gillespie, 2015)

6.7 Too Big to Fail Banks

So, if one or more of the top banks were to collapse, the U.S. may have to face serious financial consequences. However, the current standing of these banks in the economy makes them *"too big to fail"* (TBTF). In other words, the U. S. government has to bail them out should they face financial crisis – but the Federal Reserve needs money for that too! (Sorkin, 2010), (Stern, 2009)

Back in 2015, the Federal Reserve implemented a new rule that limits their capacity to loan emergency money to the commercial banks. From the looks of it, the rule is pretty straightforward – the American taxpayers aren't responsible for bailing out a bank that collapses. The Federal Reserve's rule allows it to ascertain, by its own measures, whether or not a bank qualifies for emergency assistance. (Gillespie, 2015)

Given that, if one or more of these TBTF banks were to go into bankruptcy because of a derivatives crisis, it would be interesting to see where the money to bail them out comes from. Or, in a worst-case scenario, will there be enough money in the economy to loan it to them if and when a crisis strikes. Or another scenario, as explained in (Mack, 2016), is that the money comes from the banks' customers via a *bail-in*.

6.8 Chapter Wrap-Up

In this chapter, we discuss the assets and liabilities of banks in the U.S. To accomplish this task, we discussed the following:

- ❖ The Economic Functions of Banks
- ❖ The Federal Reserve Bank
- ❖ Commercial and Investment Banks
- ❖ Top 25 Banks in the U.S. Based on Total Assets
- ❖ Analysis of the Federal Reserve's Balance Sheet
- ❖ Derivatives: Cause of the Proliferation of Debt in the U.S. Banking System
- ❖ "Too Big To Fail" Banks

Now, we have been going on and on about derivatives. It's true that we gave you a slight introduction to them in the beginning of the book, but to understand their complete impact on the economy, we need to take a deeper look into the subject and how they work. Let's move on to Chapter 7 for that.

Chapter 7. Derivatives

7.1 What Is a Derivative?

We defined and briefly discussed derivatives in the Preface and in Chapter 6. Many experts think that banks' overexposure to derivatives contracts led to the catastrophic economic collapse in 2008 and subsequent bank bailouts. Now, we wish to further explore derivatives in this chapter and to understand their relevance to the U.S. debt.

For anyone who has been a part of the investment markets in the U.S., the term *derivative* is not a new one. A derivative is a financial contract that is linked to another security – bonds and stocks being the most common ones. These derivatives get their value from the value of the underlying security they are linked to. In simple words, derivatives, on their own, aren't worth anything at all. *So how do they work and why do people invest in them?* Let's find out.

7.2 Types of Derivatives

There is a plethora of different types of derivatives contracts available in the market. However, the investment market and its usual financial engineering strategies, usually orbit around those listed in Table 7.1.

Table 7.1: Types of Derivatives Contracts

Type of Derivative	Definition
Futures	*Futures are financial derivatives contracts obligating the buyer to purchase an asset or the seller to sell an asset, such as a physical commodity or a financial instrument, at a predetermined future date and price.* (Investopedia, 2017g)
Options	*An options contract is a financial derivatives contract sold by one party (option writer) to another party (option holder). The options contract offers the option holder the right, but not the obligation, to buy or sell an underlying asset at an agreed-upon price during a certain period or on a specific date.* *Note: Depending on the type of options contract, this period could be days, weeks, months, or even a couple of years.* (Investopedia, 2017h), (Mack, 2016)
Swaps	*A swap is a derivative contract through which two parties exchange financial instruments. These instruments can be almost anything, but most swaps involve cash flows based on a notional principal amount that both parties agree to.* (Investopedia, 2017i)

For a more extensive discussion on the various types of derivatives contracts, please see (Duarte, 2008), (Mack, 2014), (Mack, 2016).

7.3 Example of a Derivative

For our readers who may not be that familiar with derivatives, we will now illustrate options - one of the types of derivatives defined in Table 7.1. Options can be written on many different types of underlying assets, such as stocks, commodities, foreign currencies, even real estate. In this example, we will focus on *stock options*—that is, options contracts whose underlying assets are stocks. (Mack, 2016), (OCC, 1994), (OIC, 2016)

With stock options, it is possible for investors to

- ❖ Profit whether a stock's price goes up, down, or remains flat
- ❖ Cut losses
- ❖ Protect gains
- ❖ Control a large number of shares of stocks with a relatively small cash outlay

Please note that stock options are relatively complex and may be riskier than some other financial assets. Depending on the type of stock options contract bought or sold, an investor may lose his/her entire investment.

There are two basic types of stock options: **call options** and **put options** – as denoted in Table 7.2.

Table 7.2: Definition of Call and Put Options

Call Options (aka "calls")	Put Options (aka "puts")
For each call options contract an investor purchases, he/she has the right (but not the obligation) to purchase 100 shares of a stock at a specific price within a specific time frame.	For each put options contract an investor purchases, he/she has the right (but not the obligation) to sell 100 shares of a stock at a specific price within a specific time frame.
In essence, the investor has the right to "call" stock away from someone.	In essence, the investor has the right to "put" stock to someone.

In both the case of calls and puts, the buyer (options holder) has freedom to decide whether or not to exercise the options contract. The buyer of the options contract will exercise it if it benefits him/her. Such benefits are determined by market conditions, the price of the underlying stock, and the terms of the options contract.

In Figure 7.1, we give a specific example of a call option whose underlying asset is the stock of Alibaba Group Holding Limited (NYSE:BABA). (Clark, 2016), (Mack 2016), (TradeStation)

Figure 7.1: Example of a call option whose underlying asset is the stock of Alibaba Group Holding Limited (NYSE: BABA)

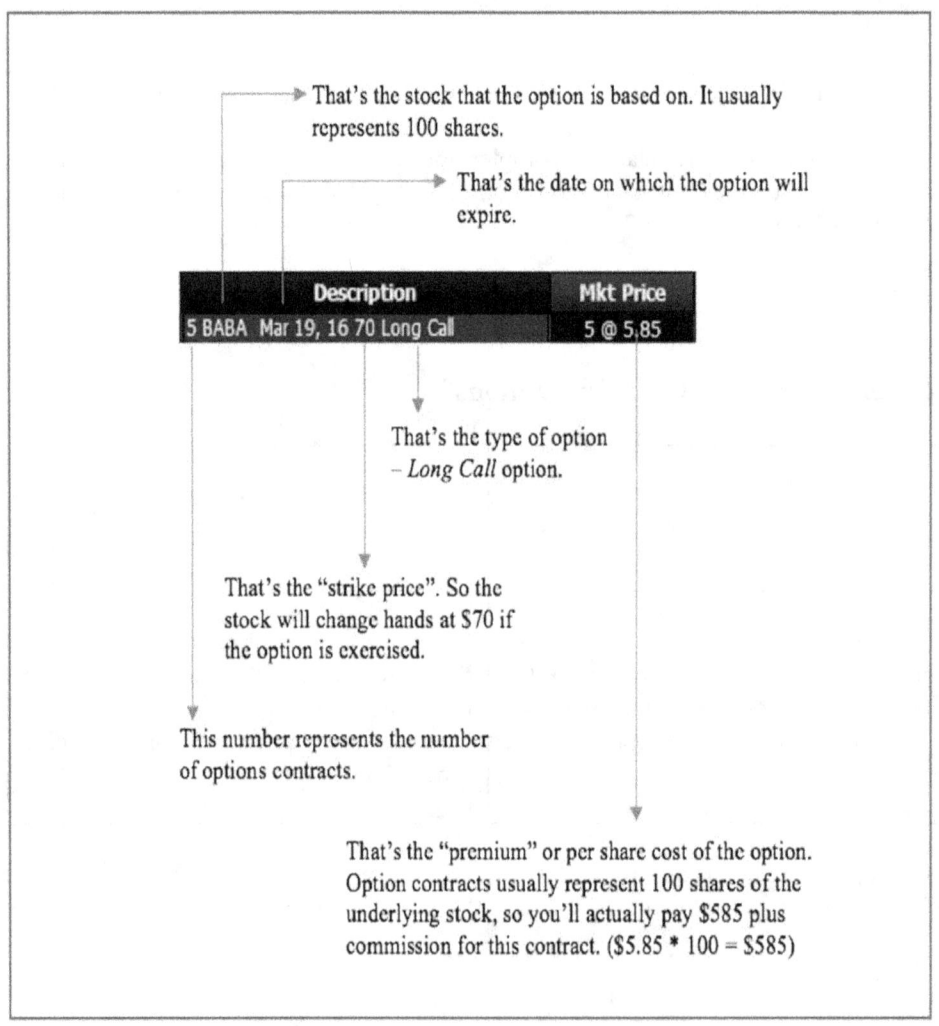

Now, let's analyze the following three scenarios in Table 7.3 to gain a bit of intuition about this call stock option illustrated in Figure 7.1.

Table 7.3: Scenarios of BABA stock prices with respect to the buy call options strategy (Mack, 2016)

Scenario #1	Scenario #2	Scenario #3
BABA drops below $70 per share	**BABA is between $70 and $75.85 per share**	**BABA is higher than $75.85 per share**
In this scenario, the call options contract can be viewed as an "insurance" policy. Had the investor bought the 500 shares of BABA instead of the 5 options contracts, she would have paid $34,915 plus commission versus $2,925 plus commission. If there was a large drop in the BABA stock price, then the investor could have lost a substantial amount of money – perhaps much more than the $2,925 plus commissions paid for the 5 call options contract. Having bought the 5 call options contracts instead, she only loses the options premium paid.	The investor will still lose money if she exercises these 5 call options. Why? Because she paid $5.85/share for them. Hence, she only begins to make money if the price of a share of Alibaba's stock is higher than $75.85/share. To use options terminology, this $75.85 is referred to as the breakeven point for her options position. Please note that the breakeven point is defined as the market price that a stock must reach for an option buyer to avoid a loss if they exercise the option. For a call buyer, the breakeven point is the strike price plus the premium paid.	The investor will finally start to make a profit when BABA is higher than $75.85 plus commission. The higher the price of BABA, the more she stands to gain from buying the 5 call options contracts.

Well, hopefully this example of a call option illustrates the complexity of derivatives. For many other examples of derivatives contracts, please see (Mack, 2014) and (Mack, 2016).

7.4 Benefits of Derivatives

As made evident from the previous definitions and example in this chapter, derivatives are financial instruments investors may use to hedge (manage) their risks. However, what most investors fail to acknowledge is the fact that risk can be hedged – but not necessarily eliminated. Keeping this harsh truth aside, derivatives still work as effective tools for investors to safeguard themselves from too much exposure to market risk.

In addition, some derivatives bring in a host of other benefits for investors, such as:

➢ <u>Some Derivatives Are Non-Binding Contracts</u>: The purchase of a derivative contract entitles an investor the right to use it. However, in most cases, these derivatives do not put an investor under the compulsion to exercise that right. As a result, derivatives bring flexibility in investment strategies for seasoned investors.

➢ <u>Derivatives Can Be Used to Leverage Returns</u>: Often investors enter the stock market in the hopes of doubling their wealth quickly. It's true, when you play your cards right, the stock market has the potential to payback substantially high returns, but even that could take years. With derivatives however, the same amount of investment can be doubled and sometimes tripled within much shorter periods – via savvy trading or even luck. Derivatives allow investors to control large positions for little amount of outlay or even nothing at all. (Investment & Finance, 2017)

With these benefits of trading derivative contracts in their portfolios, investors have a variety of investment options they can consider to grow the size of their wealth. Normally, investors can choose to trade their derivatives in two different derivatives markets:
➢ *Exchange-Traded Derivatives Markets*
➢ *Over-The-Counter (OTC Derivatives Markets)*

Let's take a look at these derivatives markets in the next two sections of this chapter.

7.5 Exchange-Traded Derivatives Markets

Exchange-traded derivatives are probably familiar to many individual investors. However, before we proceed to discuss them, let's first properly define them.

> *An **exchange-traded derivative** is a financial instrument whose value is based on the value of another asset, and that trades on a regulated exchange.* (Banks, 2003), (Investopedia, 2017j)

Exchange-traded derivatives are normally used for hedging risk exposure or speculating the movements of a diverse financial asset portfolio that includes everything from currencies and interest rates to equities and commodities. Options and futures are the two most commonly used exchange-traded derivative contracts traded on global exchanges where derivatives are recognized.

Now these exchange-traded derivatives are normally utilized by retail investors (*those who buy and sell financial instruments on a small-scale/personal account*) and hedge funds, because they provide standardization and reduced risk exposure. (Investopedia, 2017j)

However, the same standardized features do not sit well with the larger organizations. What we're trying to explain here is that the standardization (regulated by the exchange) and less exposure to risk (guaranteed against default) might give a sense of security to an individual investor, but for the bigger fish in the financial markets, the same attributes would mean the lack of flexibility in trading as well as too much transparency, which can cause trouble for arbitragers.

To summarize it all, exchange-traded derivatives offer greater transparency, liquidity, stability, and of course low-risk exposure as opposed to their counterparts – the *Over-the-Counter* Derivatives.

7.6 Over-the-Counter (OTC) Derivatives Markets

Before we move on to the OTC market, let's first understand what over-the-counter derivatives are.

> ***Over-the-counter derivatives*** *are private contracts that are traded between two parties without going through an exchange or other intermediaries.* (The President's Working Group on Financial Markets, 2015), (Investopedia, 2017k)

As you can see, no regulatory authority monitors the transactions of over-the-counter derivatives. This makes it easier for investors *(mostly large organizations in this case)* to customize and negotiate derivatives to match the risk and returns each contract counterparty requires.

The OTC derivatives are traded in a decentralized market. This market is normally made up of just the buyers and the sellers, and, of course, an alternate mode of communication that brings these parties together. Since an over-the-counter market does not have any physical presence, all transactions are made over the phone or through various electronic trading mediums.

It is quite obvious that the OTC market is regulated by the dealers (read buyers and sellers). They do that by quoting the prices at which they are willing to buy and sell assets. A trade of derivatives can occur between two consenting parties without the other parties in the market knowing anything about it.

So, if we make the effort to round up the prominent traits of the OTC derivatives and markets, one thing becomes absolutely clear: they are the complete opposite of their exchange-traded counterparts. OTCs are less transparent and have to adhere to fewer regulations, which make them more flexible. However, these derivatives and markets bring extreme credit risks, and the reason for that is straightforward – they are not backed or guaranteed by clearing corporations. (Bluhm, 2010)

7.7 How Derivatives Contribute to the U.S. Debt

So far in this chapter, we've discussed the basics of derivatives, how they work, what makes them important for the investors, and the two fundamental financial markets they are traded on. But there is a very important aspect of derivatives that we have yet to discuss.

You see, derivatives are not all fun and reward. They come with their own set of pitfalls that, as mentioned earlier, can lead to possible economic downfalls. **This is "the" aspect that is supposed to tie the content of this book together – how the banks and derivatives are contributing to the staggering amount of the U.S. debt that we face, and why they form a major chunk of it!**

Ace investor Warren Buffet termed derivatives as "time bombs" and "financial weapons of mass destruction" – and he had good reason to do so. (BBC News, 2003), (Kelleher, 2008)

If you remember, in the previous chapter, we mentioned how the Federal Reserve bails out commercial banks when they hit financial crises. However, not many people are aware of the countless times the Federal Reserve actually did so.

As discussed in (Mack, 2016), the biggest bank bailout ever conducted in the history of the world was conducted by the Federal Reserve following the 2008 subprime mortgage crises that hit the nation back then. The move was kept secret from the U.S. taxpayers and the Federal Reserve went to great lengths in fighting courts to uphold this information as a secret. (Table 7.3)

Table 7.3: Bailouts from the Federal Reserve to American and Foreign Banks (Mack, 2016)

Dollar in billions

Borrowing Parent Company	TAF	PDCF	TSLF	CPFF	Subtotal	AMLF	TALF	Total loans
Citigroup Inc.	$110	$2,020	$348	$33	$2,511	$1	-	$ 2,513
Morgan Stanley	-	1,913	115	4	2,032	-	9	2,041
Merrill Lynch & Co.	0	1,775	166	8	1,949	-	-	1,949
Bank of America Corporation	280	947	101	15	1,342	2	-	1,344
Barclays PLC (United Kingdom)	232	410	187	39	868	-	-	868
Bear Stearns Companies, Inc.	-	851	2	-	853	-	-	853
Goldman Sachs Group Inc.	-	589	225	0	814	-	-	814
Royal Bank of Scotland Group PLC (United Kingdom)	212	-	291	39	541	-	-	541
Deutsche Bank AG (Germany)	77	1	277	-	354	-	-	354
UBS AG (Switzerland)	56	35	122	75	287	-	-	287
JP Morgan Chase & Co.	99	112	68	-	279	111	-	391
Credit Suisse Group AG (Switzerland)	0	2	261	-	262	0	-	262
Lehman Brothers Holdings Inc.	-	83	99	-	183	-	-	183
Bank of Scotland PLC (United Kingdom)	181	-	-	-	181	-	-	181
BNP Paribas SA (France)	64	66	41	3	175	-	-	175
Wells Fargo & Co.	159	-	-	-	159	-	-	159
Dexia SA (Belgium)	105	-	-	53	159	-	-	159
Wachovia Corporation	142	-	-	-	142	-	-	142
Dresdner Bank AG (Germany)	123	0	1	10	135	-	-	135
Societe Generale SA (France)	124	-	-	-	124	-	-	124
All other borrowers	1,854	146	14	460	2,475	103	62	2,639
Total	$3,818	$8,951	$2,319	$738	$15,826	$217	$71	$16,115

Source: GAO analysis of Federal Reserve System data

Several bailouts have exceeded multi-trillion dollar spending by the Federal Reserve. Many of you would already be familiar with the multi-billion dollar TARP bank bailout. However, the knowledge of the Federal Reserve Bank lending over $16 trillion to the "Too Big to Fail" U.S. and foreign banks between 2007 and 2010 – that too on rates almost as good as interest-free – is not common knowledge. **Trillions of dollars were spent on bailing out domestic and foreign banks!** Even though there is a limit on the bailout amounts now – truth is, the discretion and extent of amount for bailouts still rests with the Federal Reserve and there is not much the U.S. taxpayer can do about these bailouts. (Mack, 2016)

However, these trillions of dollars paid out in U.S. and foreign bank bailouts don't even begin to match the dollar value of outstanding derivative contracts. This is because, as we saw in Table 0.1, the top five U.S. banks are drenched with derivatives exposure worth approximately $200 trillion dollars.

Now, reflect on our discussion in Chapter 6 regarding the Federal Reserve's dismal balance sheet in light of this $16 trillion bank bailout to domestic and foreign banks!

7.8 Derivatives Pyramid: $1.5 Quadrillion-Dollar Derivatives Bubble

In the previous section, we discussed the trillions of dollars in bank bailouts from the U.S. Treasury and the Federal Reserve to domestic and foreign banks. As large as these bailouts are, they pale in comparison to the value of outstanding derivatives contracts. Well-known blogger,

Michael Snyder asks, "When is the U.S. banking system going to crash? He then proceeds to answer his question: I can sum it up in three words. Watch the derivatives." (Snyder, 2014), (Snyder, 2015)

American Economist John Exter created the "Exter's Pyramid" to organize and track the size and risk of different classes of global assets. Exter was very concerned about the astronomical levels of global debt. In Figure 7.2, you will find Exter's Pyramid updated and adapted to illustrate a "conservative" estimate of the value of outstanding derivatives contracts. This global derivatives bubble is estimated to be between $1,500 TRILLION and $1,600 TRILLION dollars. So, you see from Figure 7.2 that they don't call it a *pyramid scheme* for nothing. (Mack, 2016)

Figure 7.2 Exter's Pyramid: The $1,500 TRILLION Dollar Derivatives Bubble (Mack,2016)

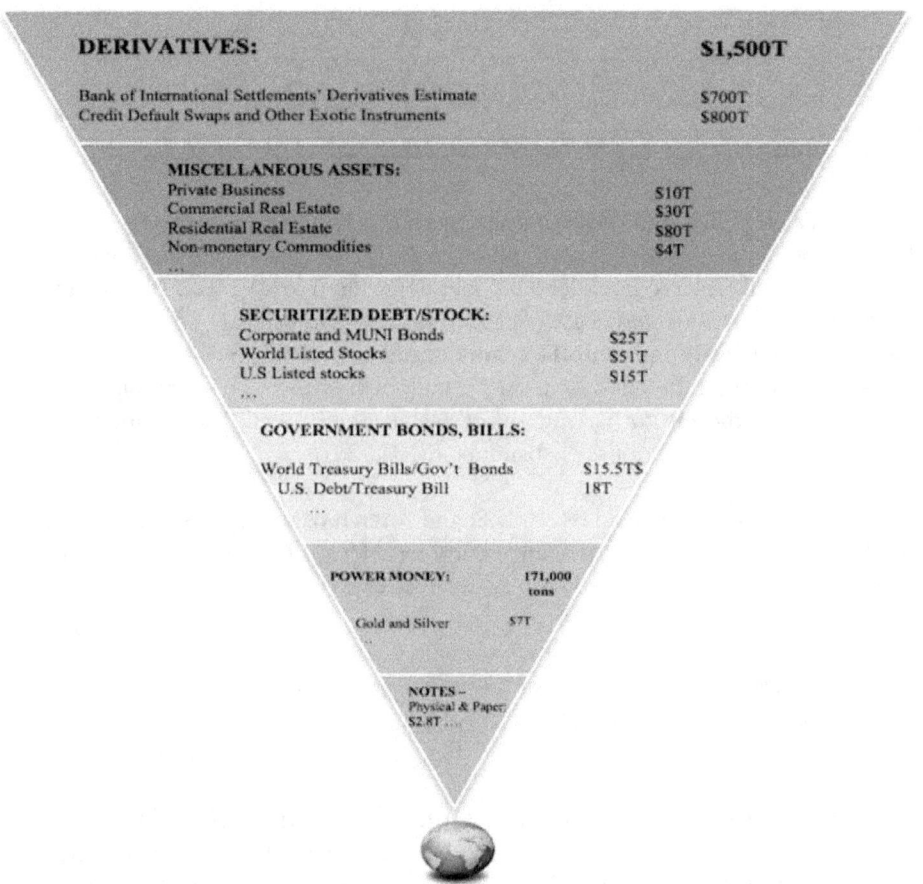

DERIVATIVES:	**$1,500T**
Bank of International Settlements' Derivatives Estimate	$700T
Credit Default Swaps and Other Exotic Instruments	$800T
MISCELLANEOUS ASSETS:	
Private Business	$10T
Commercial Real Estate	$30T
Residential Real Estate	$80T
Non-monetary Commodities	$4T
SECURITIZED DEBT/STOCK:	
Corporate and MUNI Bonds	$25T
World Listed Stocks	$51T
U.S Listed stocks	$15T
...	
GOVERNMENT BONDS, BILLS:	
World Treasury Bills/Gov't Bonds	$15.5T$
U.S. Debt/Treasury Bill	18T
...	
POWER MONEY:	171,000 tons
Gold and Silver	$7T
NOTES – Physical & Paper: $2.8T	

2016 WORLD GDP: Approximately $74 TRILLION

The derivatives exposure that our banks have makes them as good as bankrupt if markets implode. If and when this derivatives pyramid caves in, there is no way our commercial banks have what it takes to survive. The only last-resort support these financial institutions have now and probably later is the taxpayers' money that backs some of their investments in these risky assets.

7.9 Chapter Wrap-Up

In this chapter, we gave readers an introduction to the derivatives markets and their relevance to the *U.S. National Debt*. To accomplish these tasks, we discussed:

- ❖ What Is a Derivative?
- ❖ Types of Derivatives
- ❖ Example of a Derivative
- ❖ Benefits of Derivatives
- ❖ Exchange-Traded Derivatives Markets
- ❖ Over-The-Counter (OTC) Derivatives Markets
- ❖ How Derivatives Contribute to the U.S. Debt
- ❖ Derivatives Pyramid: $1.5 QUADRILLION Dollar Derivatives Bubble

Now with the overbearing clouds of debt and derivatives combined overshadowing the U.S. economy, many are concerned about whether the U.S. will ever be able to pay back or at least reduce the amount of debts it owes. The final chapter is our two cents on that.

Chapter 8. Will the U.S. Ever Be Able to Pay All of Its Debt?

Since we're going to round up the book with this chapter, it is important to have a recap of the facts and figures we already know now. The *U.S. National Debt* stands at almost $20 trillion. By far, it is the largest amount of national debt held by a country across the globe.

8.1 Previous U.S. Government Shutdowns

Since the year 2007, the U.S. debt has more or less increased by almost $1 trillion every year. That growth occurred despite many desperate attempts to stop it. There have been instances after instances when the debt crisis has exposed the U.S. to the possibility of default. There have been times when the U.S. federal government was forced to stop in its tracks (2012) and even shutdown (2013) because of debt. However, every time, the U.S. has somehow or other managed to come out of the adversity that plagues it. (Amadeo, 2017d), (Matthews, 2013)

8.2 Proposed Budget Cuts

There were attempts to limit the continuous growth of the U.S. debt ceiling. However, the *U.S. National Debt* kept increasing despite all that. Perhaps certain measures like cutting government spending, increasing taxes nationwide, and aiming for economic growth that outpaces the increase in debt can make a huge difference.

Many think that all of this falls into the category of austere measures – something many Americans, by far, aren't yet ready for. However, it seems that recent media headlines about the Trump administration's proposed budget cuts signal that such austere measures may be on the horizon.

Here are just a few examples of these headlines:

- ❖ *White House Plans to Slash Federal Jobs with Reorganization Plan* (Cordell, 2017a)
- ❖ *Trump Budget to Carve $4B From Federal Employee Retirement* (Cordell, 2017b)
- ❖ *Here Are the 66 Programs Eliminated in Trump's Budget* (Elis, 2017)
- ❖ *Trump's Budget by the Numbers: What Gets Cut and Why* (Krieg, 2017)
- ❖ *Stop Pres. Trump's Proposed Cuts to Foreign Aid* (One.Org, 2017)
- ❖ *Civil Rights Commission to Probe Potential Effects of Trump's Budget and Staffing Cuts* (Giaritelli, 2017)

To be honest, we find it quite unlikely that the U.S. will be able to pay off its debt in full - ever. Why? Just judging from the previously listed media headlines about the Trump administration's proposed budget, it seems that the Trump administration will meet with lots of resistance from many people and organizations in its attempt to tame the out-of-control national debt. Another reason behind this notion is the fact that sovereign debts – the ones owed by sovereign countries and states – become a risk only when the creditors (in this case the U.S. taxpayers) worry about not getting their money back.

8.3 U.S. Public Debt Forecasted to Grow to 150% of GDP by 2047 If No Changes Are Made

As noted on the *U.S. Debt Clock* (Figure 1.1), the gross debt-to-GDP ratio of the U.S. exceeds 100%. Even in light of this, creditors may not be too worried yet about not getting their money back. Why?

1. The U.S. bond "never" defaults.
2. The U.S. is currently the "superpower" of the world.
3. The U.S. dollar is currently the global reserve currency. (Calvo, 2014)
4. The U.S. dollar is believed to be a good long-term investment.
5. Creditors are more concerned about the publicly held debt level of the U.S. – that is, the debt the U.S. borrowed from credit markets, not the debt owed to federal trust funds such as Social Security, etc. According to the CBO, the U.S. publicly held debt currently makes up 77% of the debt-to-GDP ratio – as noted in Figure 8.1. (Boccia, 2017)

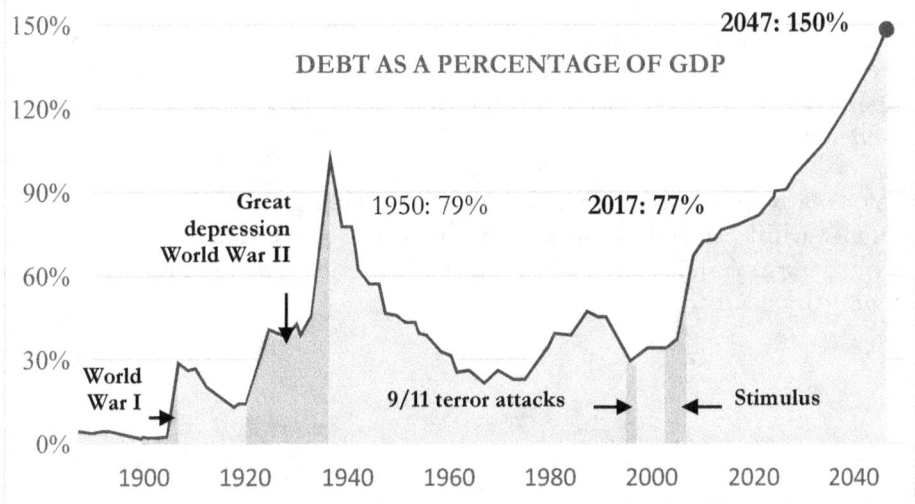

Source: Congressional Budget Office. "Budget and Economic Data." Long - Term Budget Projections, March 2017. https://www.cbo.gov/about/products/budget-economic-data#1 (accessed May 22. 2017)

According to the World Bank, trouble with the creditors begins when the ratio of the U.S. publicly held debt to the GDP ratio exceeds 77% - the current status. In addition, it has been forecasted that this ratio will skyrocket to 150% by 2047 if no drastic changes are made in our country. (Amadeo, 2017d), (Boccia, 2017), (World Bank, 2011)

8.4 Austere Economic Measures Needed to Reduce the Debt?

Coming back to why we feel the U.S. will most likely never pay off its debt in full, there are three basic reasons for that:

1. First, the popularity of senators and representatives depends on the programs they initiate and support. They usually get voted out if they make spending cuts to these programs – Medicare is one example.

2. Second, the two most effective ways of controlling and possibly reducing the debt is to either raise taxes or to cut down on government spending. Both of these methods are highly unpopular with the general public.

3. Also, over time, after World War II, the economy has dramatically outgrown the debt. Back then, even a $259 billion debt seemed too much, but it was successfully dwarfed by the economic growth that followed. Politicians believe that today's debt might bring the same impact in the years that follow.

To sum it all up, the only plausible way to reduce and possibly pay back part of the U.S. debt is to take austere measures for the same. The ideal time to do so is when the country is facing an economic boom that reduces the unemployment levels to 5% or less and there is at least 3% growth in the GDP.

In fact, it wouldn't be wrong to say that this would be the best time for such austere measures, as it may actually keep the economy from going into a recession following the boom. However, the greater question is: ***Will Americans ever be ready to face such austere economic measures?***

References

Amadeo, Kimberly, "U. S. National Debt Clock: Definition and History," The Balance, https://www.thebalance.com/u-s-national-debt-clock-definition-and-history-3306297, 2016.

Amadeo, Kimberly, "The U.S. Debt and How It Got So Big," The Balance, https://www.thebalance.com/the-u-s-debt-and-how-it-got-so-big-3305778, 2017a.

Amadeo, Kimberly, "Deficit by President: What Budget Deficits Hide," The Balance, https://www.thebalance.com/deficit-by-president-what-budget-deficits-hide-3306151, 2017b.

Amadeo, Kimberly, "Who Owns the U.S. National Debt," The Balance, https://www.thebalance.com/who-owns-the-u-s-national-debt-3306124, 2017c.

Amadeo, Kimberly, "Will the U.S. Debt Ever Be Paid Off," The Balance, https://www.thebalance.com/will-the-u-s-debt-ever-be-paid-off-3970473, 2017d.

Amadeo, Kimberly, "U. S. Debt by President: By Dollar and Percent," The Balance, https://www.thebalance.com/us-debt-by-president-by-dollar-and-percent-3306296, 2017e.

Bank of International Settlements (BIS), https://www.bis.org, 2017.

Banks, Eric, Exchange-Traded Derivatives, 1st Edition, Wiley, http://amzn.to/2t14ddE, 2003.

BBC News, Buffett warns on investment 'time bomb', http://news.bbc.co.uk/2/hi/2817995.stm, 2003.

Benston, George, The Separation of Commercial and Investment Banking: The Glass-Steagall Act Revisited and Reconsidered, Oxford University Press, http://amzn.to/2t19QrX, 1990.

Bipartisan Budget Act of 2015, Public Law 114-74, https://www.congress.gov/114/plaws/publ74/PLAW-114publ74.pdf, 2015.

Bittle, Scott, Where Does the Money Go? Rev Ed: Your Guided Tour to the Federal Budget Crisis (Guided Tour of the Economy), HarperBusiness, http://amzn.to/2tTylUF, 2011.

Bluhm, Christian, Introduction to Credit Risk Modeling, 2nd Edition, Chapman and Hall, http://amzn.to/2s1MM7K, 2010.

Board of Governors of the Federal Reserve System, "Who owns the Federal Reserve?" http://www.federalreserve.gov/faqs/about_14986.htm, 2013.

Board of Governors of the Federal Reserve System, https://www.federalreserve.gov, 2017.

Boccia, Romina, "A Fiscal Storm is Brewing: US Public Debt to Grow to 150% of GDP by 2047

If No Changes," CNS News, http://www.cnsnews.com/commentary/romina-boccia/fiscal-storm-brewing-us-public-debt-grow-150-gdp-2047-if-no-changes, 2017.

Booth, Danielle, Fed Up: An Insider's Take on Why the Federal Reserve Is Bad for America, Portfolio, http://amzn.to/2tA5N3i, 2017.

Business Dictionary, http://www.businessdictionary.com/definition/national-debt.html, 2017.

Calvo, Fabian, *The Global Economic Reset: The Day America Loses the World Reserve Currency*, CreateSpace Independent Publishing Platform, http://amzn.to/2tVfDwe, 2014.

Clark, C.E., "What Is Included in the U.S. National Debt? Who Does the U.S. Owe All That Money to?" *Hubpages*, https://hubpages.com/politics/US-national-debt-explained-what-debt-includes-why-it-is-not-a-worry, 2017.

Clark, Duncan, *Alibaba: The House That Jack Ma Built*, Ecco, http://amzn.to/2s1Qnml, 2016.

CNNMoney, *Donald Trump Says He Can "Make a Deal" on America's Debt*, http://money.cnn.com/2016/05/10/news/economy/us-debt-ownership/index.html, 2016.

Congress of the United States, Congressional Budget Office (CBO), *The 2017 Long-Term Budget Outlook*, https://www.cbo.gov/system/files/115th-congress-2017-2018/reports/52480-ltbo.pdf, 2017.

Cordell, Carten, "White House Plans to Slash Federal Jobs With Reorganization Plan," *Federal Times*, http://www.federaltimes.com/articles/white-house-plans-to-slash-federal-jobs-with-reorganization-plan, 2017a.

Cordell, Carten, "Trump Budget to Carve $4B From Federal Employee Retirement," *Federal Times*, http://www.federaltimes.com/articles/trump-budget-to-carve-4b-from-federal-employee-retirement, 2017b.

Crudele, John, "$20 trillion Debt Deserves as Much Attention as Dow Hitting 20,000," *New York Post*, http://nypost.com/2017/03/20/20-trillion-debt-deserves-as-much-attention-as-dow-hitting-20000/, 2017.

Davis, A. and J. R. Harrigan, "Debt Myths, Debunked," *U.S. News and World Report*, https://www.usnews.com/opinion/economic-intelligence/articles/2016-12-01/myths-and-facts-about-the-us-federal-debt, 2016.

Dennis, Steven T., "The Debt Ceiling," *Bloomberg*, https://www.bloomberg.com/quicktake/the-debt-ceiling, 2017.

DR. ECON, "What Is the Economic Function of a Bank?" *Federal Reserve Bank of San Francisco*, http://www.frbsf.org/education/publications/doctor-econ/2001/july/bank-economic-function/, 2001.

Duarte, Joe, *Trading Futures for Dummies*, http://amzn.to/2rXHTBA, 2008.

Durden, Tyler, "The Debt Ceiling Deadline Has Passed: Now the Biggest Test of Donald Trump's Presidency Begins…," *ZeroHedge*, http://www.zerohedge.com/news/2017-03-17/debt-ceiling-deadline-has-passed-now-biggest-test-donald-trumps-presidency-begins, 2017.

Elis, Niv, "Here Are the 66 Programs Eliminated in Trump's Budget," *The Hill*, http://thehill.com/policy/finance/334768-here-are-the-66-programs-eliminated-in-trumps-budget, 2017.

Factors Affecting Reserve Balances, Federal Reserve Statistical Release, https://www.federalreserve.gov/releases/h41/Current/, 2017.

Federal Debt Held by the Public, *Federal Reserve Economic Data (FRED)*, https://fred.stlouisfed.org/series/FYGFDPUN, 2017.

Federal Reserve Act, 1913, "Federal Reserve Bank," *Wikipedia*, https://en.wikipedia.org/wiki/Federal_Reserve_Bank, 2016.

Financial Crisis Inquiry Commission, *The Financial Crisis Inquiry Report, Authorized Edition: Final Report of the National Commission on the Causes of the Financial and Economic Crisis in the United States*, 1st Edition, http://amzn.to/2rHlyE9, 2011.

Firestone, Joseph, *Fixing the Debt Without Breaking America: Austerity, the Trillion Dollar Coin, and Ending Debt Ceiling, Sequester, and Budgetary Crises*, Amazon Digital Services LLC, http://amzn.to/2tUACiu, 2014.

Folger, Jean, "Options Pricing: Factors That Influence Option Price," Investopedia, http://www.investopedia.com/university/options-pricing/option-price-influence.asp, 2017.

Fontinelle, Amy, "Banking: Why Use a Bank?" http://www.investopedia.com/university/banking/banking1.asp, 2017.

Giaritelli, Anna, "Civil Rights Commission to Probe Potential Effects of Trump's Budget and Staffing Cuts," *Washington Examiner*, http://www.washingtonexaminer.com/civil-rights-commission-to-probe-potential-effects-of-trumps-budget-and-staffing-cuts/article/2626267, 2017.

Gillespie, Patrick, "Fed Ends 'Too Big to Fail' Lending to Collapsing Banks," CNN Money, http://money.cnn.com/2015/11/30/news/economy/fed-adopts-rule-to-end-too-big-to-fail/, 2015.

Griffin, G. Edward, *The Creature from Jekyll Island: A Second Look at the Federal Reserve*, 5th Edition, America Media, http://amzn.to/2t0F2HJ, 2010.

Hall, G. J., and T. J. Sargent, "A History of U.S. Debt Limits," *National Bureau of Economic Research*, Working Paper 21799, http://www.nber.org/papers/w21799, 2015.

Hoft, Jim, "Amazing! Trump Cuts US Debt by $12 Billion in His First Month," *Gateway Pundit*, http://www.thegatewaypundit.com/2017/02/trump-cuts-us-debt-burden-by-12-billion-in-his-first-month/, 2017.

Hull, John, *Options, Futures, and Other Derivatives* (9th Edition), Pearson, http://amzn.to/2tTbCID, 2014.

Imbert, Fred, "Dow Closes Above 20,000 for First Time as Trump Orders Send Stocks Flying," *CNBC*, http://www.cnbc.com/2017/01/25/us-markets.html, 2017.

Investment & Finance, *Derivatives and Leverage*, http://www.investment-and-finance.net/derivatives/tutorials/derivatives-and-leverage.html, 2017.

Investopedia, *What's the Difference Between Investment Banks and Commercial Banks?* http://www.investopedia.com/ask/answers/061615/whats-difference-between-investment-banks-and-commercial-banks.asp?lgl=myfinance-layout-no-ads, 2015.

Investopedia, *The National Debt Explained*, http://www.investopedia.com/updates/usa-national-debt/, 2016.

Investopedia, *Budget Deficit*, http://www.investopedia.com/terms/b/budget-deficit.asp, 2017a.

Investopedia, *Commercial Bank*, http://www.investopedia.com/terms/c/commercialbank.asp?lgl=myfinance-layout-no-ads, 2017b.

Investopedia, *Investment Bank*, http://www.investopedia.com/terms/i/investmentbank.asp?lgl=myfinance-layout-no-ads, 2017c.

Investopedia, *Price-Earnings Ratio*, http://www.investopedia.com/terms/p/price-earningsratio.asp, 2017d.

Investopedia, *Earnings Per Share*, http://www.investopedia.com/terms/e/eps.asp, 2017e.

Investopedia, *Debt/Equity Ratio*, http://www.investopedia.com/terms/d/debtequityratio.asp, 2017f.

Investopedia, *Futures*, http://www.investopedia.com/terms/f/futures.asp, 2017g.

Investopedia, *Option*, http://www.investopedia.com/terms/o/option.asp, 2017h.

Investopedia, *Swaps*, http://www.investopedia.com/terms/s/swap.asp?ad=dirN&qo=investopediaSiteSearch&qsrc=0&o=40186, 2017i.

Investopedia, *Exchange Traded Derivative*, http://www.investopedia.com/terms/e/exchange-traded-derivative.asp, 2017j.

Investopedia, *What Is an Over-the-Counter Derivative?* http://www.investopedia.com/ask/answers/052815/what-overthecounter-derivative.asp, 2017k.

Ittelson, Thomas, *Financial Statements: A Step-by-Step Guide to Understanding and Creating Financial Reports*, Press, http://amzn.to/2t0sbFT, 2009.

Kelleher, James B., "Buffett's 'Time Bomb' Goes Off on Wall Street," *Reuters*, http://www.reuters.com/article/us-derivatives-credit-idUSN1837154020080918, 2011.

Kessler, Glenn, "History Lesson: Why Did Congress Create a National Debt Limit?," *Washington Post*, https://www.washingtonpost.com/blogs/fact-checker/post/history-lesson-why-did-congress-create-a-national-debt-limit/2013/01/13/21114db8-5db8-11e2-9940-6fc488f3fecd_blog.html?utm_term=.2f4a751e04bd, 2013.

Krantz, Matthew and Robert Johnson, *Investment Banking for Dummies*, http://amzn.to/2t02VQd, 2014.

Krieg, Gregory and W. Mullery, "Trump's Budget by the Numbers: What Gets Cut and Why," *CNN Politics*, http://www.cnn.com/2017/05/23/politics/trump-budget-cuts-programs/index.html, 2017.

LeBor, Adam, *Tower of Basel: The Shadowy History of the Secret Bank That Runs the World*, PublicAffairs, http://amzn.to/2tA2rgF, 2014.

Mack, Iris Marie, *Energy Trading and Risk Management: A Practical Approach to Hedging, Trading and Portfolio Diversification*, Wiley Finance Publisher, http://amzn.to/2sUSmgH, 2014.

Mack, Iris Marie, *A Wall Street Bailout for Main Street: This Bulletproof Trade Will Help You Get Paid*, Amazon CreateSpace Independent Publishing Platform, http://amzn.to/2rGk5y6, 2016.

Major Foreign Holders of Treasury Securities, TicData.Treasury.gov, http://ticdata.treasury.gov/Publish/mfh.txt, 2017.

Matthew, Dylan, "Here Is Every Previous Government Shutdown, Why They Happened and How They Ended," *The Washington Post*, https://www.washingtonpost.com/news/wonk/wp/2013/09/25/here-is-every-previous-government-shutdown-why-they-happened-and-how-they-ended/?utm_term=.6d3ee5addf3c, 2013.

McCown, Ashby, L. Plantier and J. Weeks, "Petrodollars and Global Imbalances," *Department of the Treasury Office of International Affairs*, https://www.treasury.gov/press-center/press-releases/Documents/petrodollars.pdf, 2006.

Meyer, Ali, "Federal Debt Held by Public Now at Highest Level Since World War II," *The Washington Free Beacon*, http://freebeacon.com/issues/federal-debt-held-public-now-highest-level-since-world-war-ii/, 2017.

Monthly Treasury Statement of Receipts and Outlays of the United States Government, https://www.fiscal.treasury.gov/fsreports/rpt/mthTreasStmt/mts1216.pdf, 2017.

Moore, Ashley, "The Potential 2017 Government Shutdown Sparks Doubt for Trump Agenda," *Money Morning*, https://moneymorning.com/2017/04/07/the-potential-2017-government-shutdown-sparks-doubt-for-trump-agenda/, 2017.

Mullen, Jethro, "China Is No Longer the Biggest Foreign Holder of the U.S. Debt," *CNNMoney*, http://money.cnn.com/2016/12/16/investing/china-japan-us-debt-treasuries/index.html, 2016.

National Debt Clocks, http://www.nationaldebtclocks.org/debtclock/unitedstates, 2017.

Office of the Comptroller of the Currency (OCC), https://www.occ.treas.gov, 2017.

One.org, *Stop Pres. Trump's Proposed Cuts to Foreign Aid*, https://www.one.org/us/action/us_budget_trump_petition/?gclid=Cj0KEQjwg47KBRDk7LSu4LTD8eEBEiQA O4O6r5vMhUDPIFLj927TEYqSFL9PF7N6XJAOk-VYoB3-3csaAovq8P8HAQ, 2017.

Options Clearing Corporation (OCC), *Characteristics and Risks of Standardized Options*, http://www.optionsclearing.com/components/docs/riskstoc.pdf, 1994.

Options Industry Council (OIC), *Options Education Program*, http://www.optionseducation.org/en.html, 2016.

Patton, Mike, "U.S. Debt Is Heading Toward $20 Trillion: Where It's Been, Where It's Going and Why," *Forbes*, https://www.forbes.com/sites/mikepatton/2016/03/28/u-s-debt-is-heading-toward-20-trillion-where-its-been-where-its-going-and-why/#402b04817a25, 2017.

Piper, Mike, *Accounting Made Simple: Accounting Explained in 100 Pages or Less*, Simple Subjects, LLC, http://amzn.to/2s0oH1v, 2010.

Prestbo, John, *The Market's Measure: An Illustrated History of America Told Through the Dow Jones Industrial Average*, Dow Jones & Company, Inc., http://amzn.to/2t16u8k, 1999.

Rothbard, Murray, *The Mystery of Banking*, 2nd Edition, Ludwig von Mises Institute, http://amzn.to/2s1egdK, 2008.

Sartre, "Raising the Ides of March Debt Limit," *Veterans News Now*, http://www.veteransnewsnow.com/2017/03/14/raising-the-ides-of-march-debt-limit/, 2017.

Savransky, Rebecca, "Mnuchin Vows Debt Limit Won't Become Crisis," *The Hill*, http://thehill.com/policy/finance/330604-mnuchin-on-debt-limit-were-not-going-to-let-this-become-an-issue, 2017.

Smith, Allen, *RAIDING THE TRUST FUND: Using Social Security Money to Fund Tax Cuts for the Rich*, Ironwood Publications, http://amzn.to/2fhO7GQ, 2015.

Smith, Benjamin, "Debt Ceiling Crisis 2017: Profound Consequences If No Solution Found," *Lombardi Letter*, https://www.lombardiletter.com/debt-ceiling-crisis-2017-profound-consequences-no-solution-found/9871/, 2017.

Snyder, Michael, "The U.S. National Debt Has Grown by More Than a Trillion Dollars in the Last 12 Months." *The Economic Collapse,* http://theeconomiccollapseblog.com/archives/the-u-s-national-debt-has-grown-by-more-than-a-trillion-dollars-in-the-last-12-months, 2014.

Snyder, Michael, "Financial Armageddon Approaches: U. S. Banks Have 247 Trillion Dollars of Exposure to Derivatives." *The Economic Collapse.* http://theeconomiccollapseblog.com/archives/financial-armageddon-approaches-u-s-banks-have-247-trillion-dollars-of-exposure-to-derivatives, 2015.

Sorkin, Andrew, *Too Big to Fail: The Inside Story of How Wall Street and Washington Fought to Save the Financial System-and Themselves*, Penguin Books, http://amzn.to/2t1KQ3J, 2010.

Stern, Gary, *Too Big to Fail: The Hazards of Bank Bailouts*, Brookings Institution Press, http://amzn.to/2t1n9IO, 2009.

Sutch, Richard, "Liberty Bonds," *Federal Reserve History*, https://www.federalreservehistory.org/essays/liberty_bonds, 2017.

Thau, Annette, *The Bond Book, Third Edition: Everything Investors Need to Know About Treasuries, Municipals, GNMAs, Corporates, Zeros, Bond Funds, Money Market Funds, and More (Professional Finance & Investment)*, McGraw-Hill Education, http://amzn.to/2rWJZlb, 2010.

The Concord Coalition, "Understanding the Federal Debt Limit," http://www.concordcoalition.org/issue-briefs/2017/0316/understanding-federal-debt-limit, 2017.

The Debt to the Penny and Who Holds It, https://www.treasurydirect.gov/NP/debt/current, 2017.

The President's Working Group on Financial Markets, Over-the-Counter Derivatives Markets and the Commodity Exchange Act, CreateSpace Independent Publishing Platform, http://amzn.to/2rIEJNV, *2015.*

Thomas, Ken and Josh Boak, "President Trump Launches $1 Trillion Initiative to Fix America's Infrastructure," *Time*, http://time.com/4805666/donald-trump-infrastructure-roads-bridges-planes-plan/, 2017.

Thomsett, Michael, *Getting Started in Options*, Wiley, http://amzn.to/2sZYbJY, 2013.

TradeStation, www.TradeStation.com

Treasury Bulletin, https://www.fiscal.treasury.gov/fsreports/rpt/treasBulletin/current.htm, 2017.

TreasuryDirect, https://treasurydirect.gov, 2017a.

TreasuryDirect, *Frequently Asked Questions About the Public Debt*, https://www.treasurydirect.gov/govt/resources/faq/faq_publicdebt.htm, 2017b.

TreasuryDirect, *Intragovernmental Holdings and Debt Held by the Public,* https://www.treasurydirect.gov/govt/charts/principal/principal_govpub.htm, 2017c.

TreasuryDirect, *Debt Position and Activity Report,* https://www.treasurydirect.gov/govt/reports/pd/pd_debtposactrpt_0517.pdf, 2017d.

Trump, Donald J. and Tony Schwartz, *Trump: The Art of the Deal,* Ballantine Books, http://amzn.to/2sZzzBk, 2015.

U.S. Debt Clock, http://www.usdebtclock.org, 2017.

U.S. Department of Treasury, Bureau of the Public Debt, https://www.publicdebt.treas.gov, 2017.

Watson, Mark, *Department of the Treasury (Know Your Government),* Chelsea House Pub, http://amzn.to/2s0Gjdgm, 1989.

World Bank, *A Guide to the World Bank,* http://amzn.to/2s1LPN5, 2011.

About the Author and Co-Authors

Author Iris Mack, PhD, EMBA is an American academic, author, and entrepreneur who has focused on risk management and energy derivative products in the trading market. She is a former professor at MIT and currently lectures for Fitch Learning Certificate in Quantitative Finance Programme on Wall Street. Dr. Mack has also worked for prestigious organizations, such as AT&T Bell Labs, NASA, and Boeing. More information about Dr. Mack may be found on her Amazon Author page and in her finance and business columns for the International Business Times – UK edition.

Co-Author Jiayi Chen, MS is a Securities Lending Operations Analyst at Sumitomo Mitsui Trust Bank (U.S.A). He has profound experiences on Equities Lending, Risk Management, M&A, Private Equity, Data Analytics, and Financial Platform Development. Previously, he worked for multiple Financial Industry companies as a business researcher and valuation analyst. He received his MS in Finance from Tulane University and his MS in Actuarial Science from Columbia University.

Co-Author Junbo Zhu, MS is a very detail-oriented individual with a solid academic background and excellent analytical skills. He received his Master of Management in Energy and Bachelor degree in Finance from Tulane University. Junbo also specializes in risk management and asset management.

Other Books by Author Iris Marie Mack, PhD, EMBA

Energy Trading and Risk Management: A Practical Approach to Hedging, Trading and Portfolio Diversification (Wiley Finance), 1st Edition

A Wall Street Bailout for Main Street: This Bulletproof Trade Will Help You Get Paid

Mama says, "Money Doesn't Grow on Trees!": World of Dr. Mackamatix Mathematics Edutainment Book

Rescate de Wall Street Para Main Street: La Estrategia Blindala Que Sera' Bien Pagada (Spanish Edition)

INDEX